MW01284997

Baseball Games

Home Versions
of the National Pastime
1860s-1960s

Mark Cooper, M.D.

with Douglas Congdon-Martin

Special Contributions by Vincent F. Hink and William E. Howard

Price Guide

Dedication

To the memory of my father, who shared with me his love of baseball. To my mother who enabled me to pursue my passion. To my children, Michelle and Noah, who have helped remind me of the joy of game playing. And especially to my wife, Lynne, whose encouragement, understanding, and love has enabled me to accomplish this labor of love.

Printed in the Hong Kong
ISBN: 0-88740-767-6

Library of Congress Cataloging-in-Publication Data

Cooper, Mark W.
　　Baseball games: home versions of the national pastime, 1860-1980/Mark W. Cooper with Douglas Congdon-Martin: special contributions by Vincent F. Hink and William E. Howard.
　　　　p.　cm.
Includes bibliographical references and index.
　　ISBN 0-88740-767-6 (hard)
　　1. Board games--United States--History. 2. Baseball--United States--History. 3. Card games--United States--History.
I. Congdon-Martin, Douglas. II. Title
GV1312.C66　1995
794'.0216--dc20　　　　　　　　　95-1297
　　　　　　　　　　　　　　　CIP

Acknowledgments

The Coin-Op chapter could not have been completed without the aid of Phill Emmert's flyers and advertisements, Mike Brown's collection and photographs, and especially Bill Howard's collection, knowledge, and writing.

The All-Star baseball chapter was completely written by Vince Hink. All pictures are from his collection.

I also thank Marty and Debby Krim for sharing their collection and to Marty for his assistance in producing an accurate price guide that reflects today's market.

Other contributors include Barry Sloate, Patrice McFarland, Doug Palmieri, Bob Richardson, Bruce Dorskind, Howard Pollack, M.D., Roy and Grace Olsen, Roger Burbank, and John Thorn. My brother, Harry Cooper, M.D., read the manuscript and made helpful suggestions.

Mark Balbach and Doug Congdon-Martin did the bulk of the photography of my collection, with many of the aforementioned providing beautiful photographs of their collections. Jean Cline had the nearly impossible task of transcribing tape recordings of the text. Ellen J. (Sue) Taylor designed the book.

Published by Schiffer Publishing, Ltd.
77 Lower Valley Road
Atglen, PA 19310
Please write for a free catalog.
This book may be purchased from the publisher.
Please include $2.95 postage.
Try your bookstore first.

We are interested in hearing from authors
with book ideas on related subjects.

Contents

Preface

Timelessness, the lack of a clock to signal the end of the game, is part of the uniqueness and beauty of baseball, parlor games, and childhood itself. Baseball is the ideal sport to be captured in a board or card game, because, in both, time is not a factor.

When I was a child, I played my favorite baseball board game hour after hour. The roll of the dice or the spin of the wheel was enough to fill an afternoon with enjoyment. These old games are now an anachronism. Today, my children are attracted to the realism and excitement of the computer driven video game. The action of the board game is too slow to keep their interest.

Times have changed. My childhood was a time when baseball cards rattled in bicycle spokes or were flipped on sidewalks or against street corners. Today they are placed in plastic screw cases and held by 8 year old investors, hoping that their value will increase. Then we traded player's cards because a player was our favorite; he was a hero to a young little league first baseman, and we lived and died with his every game. Now a player's card is traded because of its value in the most recent baseball card price guide.

Baseball board and table games were played by children, and adults wanting to relive their childhood. They were used to replicate action on the field, to nurture our fantasy about being the major leaguers we idolized. The games were played on living room floors when living rooms were actually lived in, not decorated and treated as museums.

The baseball games presented in this book have endured countless hours of rolling dice or flicking a spinner with just the right touch to get the desired result. These games speak of the innocence of baseball, before it was a big business. They recall a simpler time of childhood, when an acquired major league game-used bat or autographed ball was not encased in a plastic showcase, but taken to a local field and used for its real purpose...playing ball.

These baseball games also reflect the history and evolution of the game. Here you will find the 19th century rule changes, the golden era when superstars did not gaze at their home runs from home plate, but ran, not walked around the bases, when autographs were freely given at the ball parks, not sold on television. This was a time when 20 game winners did not wait for their middle relievers, but pitched complete games. The baseball games depicted in this book remind us of the innocence of childhood and baseball.

Unlike baseball cards, these games are not common items. Relative to cards, the original number of games produced was small, and, because of their daily usage, few remain and still fewer have survived in displayable condition. While the pages of baseball trade publications are packed with hundreds of thousands of cards, bats, balls, and other types of memorabilia, one can search for months without discovering one pre-World War II baseball game. It is because of their true rarity and the lack of documentation of these treasures of baseball that I undertook to publish this book. It is a labor of love, that I hope will not only be a valued reference book for baseball games, but will remind all of us of a time when baseball was only a Game.

Categorizing baseball games by century, and by player-endorsed or non-endorsed, is a way of helping the collector understand the various types of games. Although there is overlap between card, action, and board games, hopefully the segregation of these games will be helpful in organizing one's thoughts about the games.

I chose an arbitrary cut-off date of the 1950s for most games, except for the player-endorsed variety. I apologize to all the Stratomatic and A.P.B.A. fans, but I feel that the inclusion of All-Star Baseball will mollify most.

Introduction

The nineteenth century in the United States was a time of dramatic social change. Immigration, industrialization, and urbanization brought new stresses and opportunities to a growing middle class. In the midst of this sometimes chaotic change, the home became an oasis of tranquility. In the home, the parlor became the place where the family would retreat. There they would interact and relax, finding entertainment in the form of books, toys, and games. The need to fulfill this need for parlor entertainment was the impetus for the birth of a new industry: the American game company.

W. & S.B. Ives Company began as a Salem, Massachusetts, stationer. In the early 1840s it started to produce card and board games. The games were spectacularly lithographed, as one would expect from the future partner in Currier & Ives, whose art documented and mythologized eighteenth century American life.

McLoughlin Brothers was established in 1828 in New York City as a printing company. In the mid-1850s it began to compete with Ives in the board game market. Other early game manufacturers were J.H. Singer, Bliss, E.I. Horseman, Milton Bradley, and Parker Brothers.

During this initial period all games were hand-painted. This was a tedious, time consuming process, though it produced beautiful games. The design was lithographed in black ink, and the colors were added by hand. Mass-production would wait for the invention of new technologies, including the advent of chromolithography.

Lithography is a technique in which a grease crayon is used to draw images on a finely grained limestone. The crayoned section attracts ink and repels water, while the empty region does the opposite, repelling the ink and attracting the water. An image drawn in reverse on the limestone can produce hundreds of printed images on a smooth and level surface. The idea of using color was introduced in Europe in the 1830s and brought to America in 1839 by a Boston printer, William Sharp. In chromolithography multiple plates were made for each image, each for a different color of ink. These color plates, which were printed on paper on top of each other, had to be perfectly aligned on the paper or the entire print would be indistinct.

Many consider McLoughlin Brothers the most successful game manufacturer of the nineteenth century. This was due to their ability to achieve intricate detail with the chromolithographic technology. They entered into the mass production of games without a significant loss of detail and beauty.

The rising popularity of the parlor game coincided with the growth in organized baseball. The growing urbanization of America and the burgeoning industrial revolution, resulted in a society that was radically different from the agrarian society of past generations. People were living in neighborhoods, with far more social interaction than their country cousins. Industrial work, though certainly demanding, was not as time-consuming as farm labor. There was an increase in leisure time, and citizens were anxious to find recreational and cultural activities to fill the void.

At the same time that the family was discovering the delights of games in the parlor, social clubs were formed in the neighborhoods. They were the source of relaxation and fellowship, and athletic competition was a natural part of their existence. One of the most popular of the games played at the clubs was baseball.

The Rise of Baseball

Baseball in the 1840s and 1850s was quite different from the game we know today. In fact, tracing baseball's history is quite controversial. As early as the 14th century stool ball was played, in which the stalker, holding a stick in hand, defended a stool behind him. As the stools increased to four they were called bases. The term baseball was used in the 1700s by various authors.

In 18th century New England, a game called "Bound Ball" was limited to two players. One person threw the ball against a wall and the other struck at the rebounding ball with his bat. If he hit it successfully he tried to run to the wall and back before his opponent recovered the ball and hit him with it. The players switched places after the batter was put out, so each one had his own "inning."

The game of "Old Cat" utilized a wooden "cat" shaped like a spindle which was placed on the ground and "cat"-apulted in the air with a foot. The batter struck at it with a stick. As more children would play, one old cat had a batter, pitcher and two bases whereas 2, 3 and 4 old cat would simply add to the number of bases and batsmen, respectively.

In 19th century England, a game called "Rounders" was played. This early form of baseball had four stations, or bases, and one hitting area. The defensive team had a "feeder" who pitched the ball toward the hitting area, which was a hole. The batsmen then hit the ball and ran to the nearest station, and all around if possible. The fielders were "scouts" who could put the batter out by hitting him with the ball or throwing the ball in the hole (the batting position, or fifth station). This was called "grounding." When the batter made the rounds of all four stations and back to the hole or hitting station, it counted as one point. As you will see later, this game is very similar to the town ball, round ball, or the Massachusetts (New England) game, which was a predecessor to the New York game or baseball as we know it today.

The 1834 Book of Sports, published in Boston, Massachusetts, speaks of base, round, or goal ball. In this game, four stakes or stones are placed 12 to 20 yards apart, with another placed in the center. The person at the center point, tosses the ball gently to a batter, who tries to hit it. If he is successful, the player runs in a clockwise fashion around the stakes; in today's terms it would be as if he were running from third, second, first base to home plate. The batter was out if he missed the ball three times, or if the hit ball was caught by a fielder.

The 1839 Boy's Book of Sports, published in Newton, Connecticut, is the first book to state that a runner would proceed counter clockwise.

Town Ball, the Massachusetts or New England game, varied from the New York game in that the batter stood at a position halfway between first base and fourth base or home, creating what in effect was a fifth base. The Pocket Companion, a book published in the late 1850s and early 1860s, describes the game.

The appearance of the game of baseball, as we know it today, can be better described as an evolution than as a birth. For many years it was thought that the inventor was Abner Doubleday. While baseball may have evolved, the Doubleday story was born

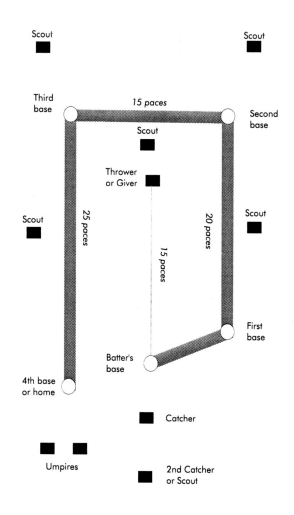

The Massachusetts Game

A diagram of the Massachusetts game playing field, adapted from *The Pocket Companion*.

in the minds of the Mills Commission. Albert G. Spalding, a former professional player, was the president of the Chicago Baseball Club and the head of a thriving sporting goods business. It could be safely said that he was the greatest baseball promoter of all time. Looking for a way to spread the good will of baseball (and increase the sales of the equipment he manufactured), in 1889 he put together a team of all-stars to tour the world and spread the gospel of "the American National Game." McLoughlin's board game, "The World's Game of Baseball," commemorates this world tour, and is probably one of the few known McLoughlin games to actually commemorate an historical sporting event.

Spalding wanted to promote baseball as an "all-American" game, the American gift to the world. He was challenged about this by Henry Chadwick, the first great sports writer to follow baseball. Chadwick, who had been born in England, believed that Cricket and Rounders were actually the predecessors to baseball. To prove the games's American roots, Spalding assigned a special commission headed by Mr. A.G. Mills, the third president of the National League, to get to the bottom of it. With Morgan G. Bulkley, the first president of the National League, Arthur P. Gorman, a senator from Maryland, N.E. Young, the fourth president of the National League, Alfred J. Reach, of Philadelphia, George Wright, probably one the most famous baseball players, and James E. Sullivan, the Mills Commission went about "investigating" the history of baseball. It issued a report in 1907 which stated that Abner Doubleday had invented the game in 1839, near Cooperstown, New York. Doubleday, who had graduated from West Point and fired the first shot at Ft. Sumter in the Civil War was just the kind of American hero the game needed. Unfortunately, at the time he was supposed to be inventing the American game at Cooperstown, he was a cadet at West Point. This did not prevent his name from being associated with the game for over 100 years. In 1939, the myth was exploited even further

to commemorate the centennial of the origin of baseball. In 1947, Robert Henderson's book, *Ball, Bat & Bishop*, disproved the myth and gave credit to the real driving force behind the modern game of baseball, Alexander Cartwright.

In the spring of 1845, Alexander Cartwright proposed the formation of a social-baseball club in New York. On September 23, 1845, the Knickerbockers Base Ball Club was formed. Drawing from earlier versions like Round Ball and Cat Ball, Cartwright drew up the rules by which his team would play. One reason the rules received broad acceptance may be that the Knickerbockers refused to play any game that was not governed by their rules.

The rules included the following.

1. Members must strictly observe the time agreed upon for exercise, and punctual in their attendance.
2. When assembled for exercise, the President, or in his absence, the Vice-President, shall appoint an Umpire, who shall keep the game in a book provided for that purpose, and note all violations of the By-Laws and Rules during the time of exercise.
3. The presiding officer shall designate two members as Captains, who shall retire and make the match to be played, observing at the same time that the players opposite to each other should be as nearly equal as possible, the choice of sides to be then tossed for, and the first in hand to be decided in like manner.
4. The bases shall be from "home" to second base, forty-two paces; from first to third base, forty-two paces, equidistant.
5. No stump match shall be played on a regular day of exercise.
6. If there should not be a sufficient number of members of the Club present at the time agreed upon to commence exercise, gentlemen not members may be chosen to make up the match, which shall not be broken up to take in members that may afterwards appear; but in all cases, members shall have the preference, when present, at the making of a match.
7. If members appear after the game is commenced, they may be chosen in if mutually agreed upon.
8. The game to consist of twenty-one counts, or aces; but at the conclusion an equal number of hands must be played.
9. The ball must be pitched, not thrown, for the bat.

The New York Game

A diagram of the New York Game playing field, adapted from *The Pocket Companion.*

10. A ball knocked out of the field, or outside the range of the first or third base, is foul.
11. Three balls being struck at and missed and the last one caught, is a hand out; if not caught is considered fair, and the striker bound to run.
12. If a ball be struck, or tipped, and caught, either flying or on the first bound, it is a hand out.
13. A player running the bases shall be out, if the ball is in the hands of an adversary on the base, or the runner is touched with it before he makes it to the base; it being understood, however, that in no instance is a ball to be thrown at him.
14. A player running who shall prevent an adversary from catching or getting the ball before making his base, is a hand out.
15. Three hands out, all out.
16. Players must take their strike in regular turn.
17. All disputes and differences relative to the game, to be decided by the Umpire, from which there is no appeal.
18. No ace or base can be made on a foul strike.
19. A runner cannot be put out in making one base, when a balk is made by the pitcher.
20. But one base allowed when a ball bounds out of the field when struck.

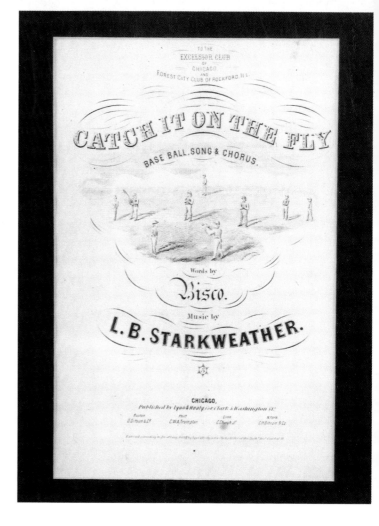

"Catch It on the Fly" sheet music. The first baseball sheet music with words, commemorating the rule change. *From the Cooper collection.*

The rules were very different from today's. In Cartwright's rules the first team with 21 runs, or aces, was the winner. The runner no longer could be out by having the ball thrown at him. Instead he had to be tagged out or have the ball ahead of him on the base. The most fortuitous decision made, as if by divine guidance, was the distance between bases. One step closer and outs would be rare; one step further and shut-outs would be commonplace.

One rule of particular interest that was often observed prior to the Civil War, gave an out when a baseball was caught on a bounce in fair or foul territory. In fact, often times, various teams would experiment with playing the game "on the fly" - having to catch the ball in the air to make an out. The first baseball sheet music with words, published in 1867, was entitled "Catch It On the Fly" to commemorate the rule change that a fair ball had to be caught on the fly.

The Knickerbocker Club team played at the Elysian Fields, across the river from New York in Hoboken, New Jersey. While the early teams were

1866 Hudson River Team photo. *From the Cooper collection.*

8

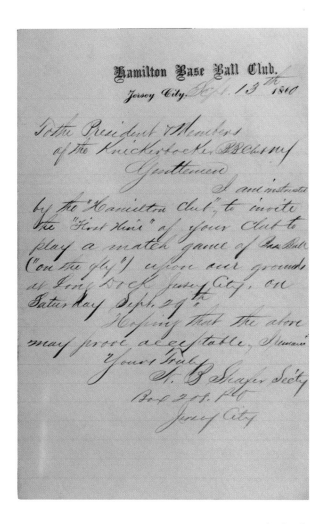

Challenge letter from the Hamilton Club to the Knickerbockers for a game played "on the fly." 1860. *From the Cooper collection.*

drawn from club members, as the popularity of the game grew their opponents came from other clubs such as the Gothams, the Putnams, or the Empires. The teams were all gentlemanly. Those members who joined were "those whose sedentary habits required recreation, and its respectability has ever been undoubted." While there was no doubt the club would welcome a player with some skill, those admitted to the club had to have "the reputation as a gentleman." The Knickerbockers could never be what was called a "match playing club" in those early days.

As the game evolved in the 1840s and 1850s, and spread south and west during the Civil War, it was purely an amateur sport. The game grew tremendously after the Civil War, with teams arising all over the country with clubs representing various institutions and areas.

The Professional Game

The amateur status was maintained until 1869, when Harry Wright formed the first professional baseball team: The Cincinnati Red Stockings. This team toured the country and in 1869 and 1870, winning an amazing 84 straight games. Finally they were defeated by the Brooklyn Atlantics in the summer of 1870 by a score of 8-7, with the Atlantics scoring three runs in the bottom of the 11th.

The Cincinnati team was led by Harry Wright, the captain and center fielder, who was paid $1200. His brother George Wright, the short stop, was paid $1400. The pitcher was Asa Brainard who earned $1100. Third baseman, Fred Waterman, was paid $1000. Charles Sweasy, the second baseman, Charles Gould, the first baseman, Douglas Allison, the catcher,

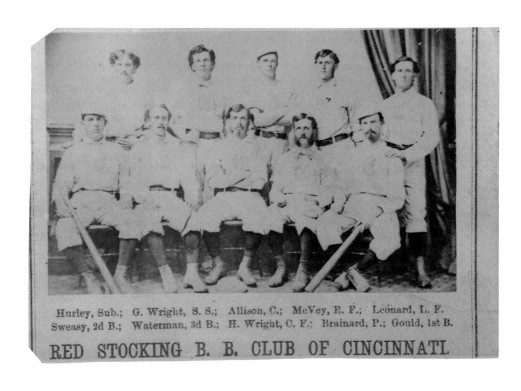

Hurley, Sub.; G. Wright, S. S.; Allison, C.; McVey, R. F.; Leonard, L. F. Sweasy, 2d B.; Waterman, 3d B.; H. Wright, C. F.; Brainard, P.; Gould, 1st B.

RED STOCKING B. B. CLUB OF CINCINNATI.

1869 Red Stockings of Cincinnati. *From the Cooper collection.*

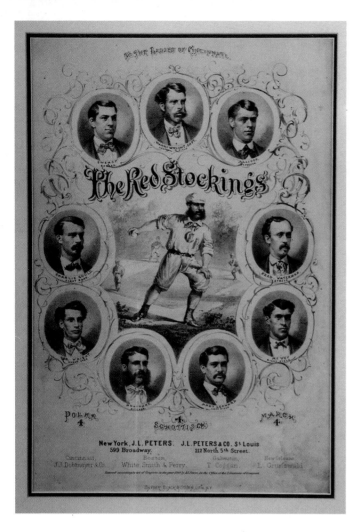

"The Red Stockings," 1869 sheet music commemorating the Cincinnati team and dedicated "To the Ladies of Cincinnati." *From the Cooper collection.*

Calvin McVey, the right fielder, and Richard Hurley, the substitute, all received a salary of $800. Andrew Leonard, the left fielder was also paid $800. And, as you can see, Andrew Leonard had played for the Hudson River team in 1866 and is the 6th gentleman from the left in the photograph.

In Rockford, Illinois, another prominent professional team, Forest Citys club, was formed. They can be seen in the accompanying carte de visite. The gentleman in the center, second from the top, was Al Spalding. Roscoe Barnes, another future hall-of-famer was seen on the right edge of the photo.

Many other teams began to pay players, and before long it became obvious that a professional baseball player's league was needed. As a natural progression The Association of Professional Base Ball Players was formed in 1871, a league organized by the players. The original member teams were the Philadelphia Athletics, the Washington Olympics, the New York Mutuals, the Unions of Troy, the Forest Cities of Rockford, the Forest Cities of Cleveland, the Chicago White Stockings, the Kekiongas of Fort Wayne. The Fort Wayne team dropped out in the inaugural season, and was replaced with the Brooklyn Eckfords.

The Boston Red Stockings were actually comprised of the remnants of Harry Wright's, 1869 Cincinnati Red Stockings team. Following their loss, the fans in Cincinnati lost interest, and by the end of the 1870 season the team was bankrupt and disbanded. From 1872 to 1875 the Boston club dominated the

The 1875 Hartford Dark Blues of the National Association. The team joined the newly formed National League in 1876. Candy Cummings was on this team. *From the Cooper collection.*

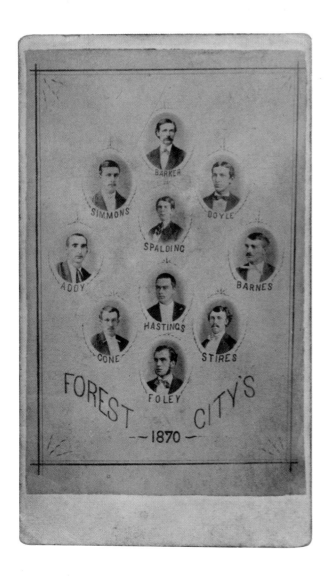

1870 Forest City Carte De Visite. Albert Spalding is in the center. *From the Cooper collection.*

PLAYED AT THE Union Grounds
On the 11 day of June, 1873.   1 hr 30 min

Boston Reds

Players' Positions.	1	2	3	4	5	6	7	8	9	10	R.	O.
G. Wright ss.	1	0	0		0	0					1	4
Barnes 3b.	1	0	1		0		0				2	3
Spalding p.	1						0				1	1
Leonard 2b.	0	0		0			0	0			0	5
White c.	0			0		0	0				3	3
O'Rourke rf.	0		0		0		1				1	3
Manning lf.		0		0		1	1				2	2
Schafer lf.		0		0		0	1				1	3
H. Wright cf.		0			0		0	1			1	3
Totals	3	0	0	0	1	1	0	4	0		9	27

Brooklyn Atlantics

Players' Positions.	1	2	3	4	5	6	7	8	9	10	R.	O.
Barlow c.	0		0	1		0			0		1	4
Pearce ss.	0		0			0			0		0	3
Burdock 2b.	0			0	4		0				0	3
Boyd rf.		0			0		0				0	2
Ferguson 3b.		0	0		0			0			0	4
Brett p.		0		1	0			0			1	3
Dehlman 1b.		1		0	0			0			1	3
Pabor lf.		0	1		0			0			1	3
Remsen cf.			0	1		0			0		1	2
Totals	0	1	0	4	0	0	0	0	0		5	27

Umpire Mr. Swandell Resolute Club

A score card from the June 11, 1873 game between the Boston Reds and the Brooklyn Atlantics. Boston won. *From the Cooper collection.*

BOSTON BASE 1873 BALL CLUB.

Association of Professional Base Ball Players. It was comprised of Harry Wright, George Wright, Andy Leonard, Charles Sweasy, from the 1869 Cincinnati Red Stockings. Added to this powerhouse team was Dave Birdsall, Harry Schafer, James Manning, Jim White, "Orator" Jim O'Rourke, Roscoe Barnes, and Al Spalding, the latter two being of the 1870 Forest Citys team.

The Boston team was a powerhouse, which may have been the undoing of the league. Other teams could not compete against this dominant force, which led to the flagging interest on the part of the fans. Contributing to the lack of fan interest was the widespread game fixing, a result of significant gambling during this time. Despite the diminished fan inter-

The 1873 Boston Base Ball Club cabinet photograph. *From the Cooper collection.*

est, players' salaries escalated. Teams began to lose money (a familiar complaint). Because the league was player owned, there was no dominant force or organization to solve the issues plaguing it, and in 1875 the Association of Professional Base Ball Players was disbanded.

In 1876, a National League was founded, which was run by the owners rather than the players. The game was now becoming a business, and one of the driving forces behind this movement was Al Spalding. In 1874 he had organized two teams to travel to England to promote the game and upon his return began to take a leading role in the American game. In 1876 he convinced William A. Hulbert, the owner of the Chicago Base Ball Club, to organize a new league. To make the Chicago team stronger, Spalding recruited teammates from Boston, Cal McVey, James White, and Roscoe Barnes. From the Philadelphia Athletics he brought Adrian C. "Cap" Anson, probably the greatest player of the 19th century. The first eight teams in the National League were Chicago, Hartford, St. Louis, Boston, Louisville, New York, Philadelphia, and Cincinnati.

In the year 1877, two minor leagues were formed, International Association, led by Candy Cummings, and the League Alliance. Neither was well funded or organized, and lasted only a short time.

Probably the most influential person in the baseball during the early professional period was Harry Wright. His influence began in the late 1850s and continued into the 1880s. His formula for success as a manager was having his players work together as a team in giving their best throughout the entire game. His impact ranged from how the game looked to how it was organized. The Cincinnati Red Stockings team was one of the first teams to replace the long pants of the old style uniform with knickers. He was able to envision baseball as a paying profession and insisted upon sobriety and good physical condition for all of his players at a time when drunkenness and laxness among players was prevalent. In 1894, when Wright retired from active duty, his contribution to baseball was expressed by Sporting Life: "Every magnate in the country is indebted to this man for the establishment of baseball as a business, and every patron for furnishing him with a systematic recreation. Every player is indebted to him for inaugurating an occupation by which he gains a livelihood, and the country at large for adding one more industry (for industry it is in one respect to furnish employment)."

Until 1882, there was no other league that was competitive with the National League. The formation of the American Association changed that. Un-

1879 cabinet photograph of Harry Wright. *From the Cooper collection.*

1888 tintype image of Harry Wright. *From the Cooper collection.*

12

1882 Chicago baseball club. *From the Cooper collection.*

der the leadership of Denny McKnight, they drew crowds with their 25 cent admission, and there location in population centers unserved by the National League. There were significant trade wars between the two leagues, with many players jumping from one to the other for a better contract. This new league was comprised of Cincinnati Reds, Philadelphia Athletics, St. Louis Browns, Louisville, Pittsburgh, and Baltimore. Cincinnati won the first championship and played a two-game series against the National League champion Chicago White Stockings. This series was not condoned officially by the National League and was split one game apiece.

During this period the National League had a reserve clause which bound a player to the team they were playing for and limited their salary. In 1883 the American Association denounced the reserve clause, hoping to have players jump to their league. To resolve the conflict this created, the president of the National League and the American Asociation president, Denny McKnight, negotiated a national agreement that recognized the American Association and adopted the reserve clause. This reserve clause actually gave the clubs a perpetual option on the player who signed with them. When a player signed his first original baseball contract, he was signing for his entire career. As Spalding acknowledged, the object of the reserve clause was "to prevent competition for the best players in each of the other clubs and to keep those clubs together." But this was obviously done at the expense of players' rights to negotiate in the open

market. In 1883 the American Association and National League agreed to let each team reserve eleven players. This was increased to fourteen in 1887, which, at that time, was almost the entire squad.

The first official world series occurred in 1884 when the Providence Grays of the National League defeated the New York Metropolitans, three games to zero. Charles "Old Hoss" Radbourn was the pitching star for the Grays, winning all three games.

Because of the reserve clause, the Union Association was formed as a rival league in 1884. Henry Lucas from St. Louis was a driving force in forming the league. The Union Association season was won handily by St. Louis which won 94 of its 113 games. Fred "Sure Shot" Dunlap led the team and the league with a .412 batting average. The other teams were Altoona, Cincinnati, Chicago, Keystones of Philadelphia, Baltimore, Boston and the Nationals of Washington. This league lasted only one year and was disbanded for financial reasons and the lack of competition.

The collapse of the Union Association again left two major leagues; the National League and American Association. In 1884, the National League advised the American Association to expand to twelve teams to combat the Union Association. This put a significant financial strain on the American Association. The American Association was wary of the National League's advice. Their suspicions grew when they found out that the National League had negotiated with the St. Louis franchise of the Union Association to come join the National League as the St. Louis

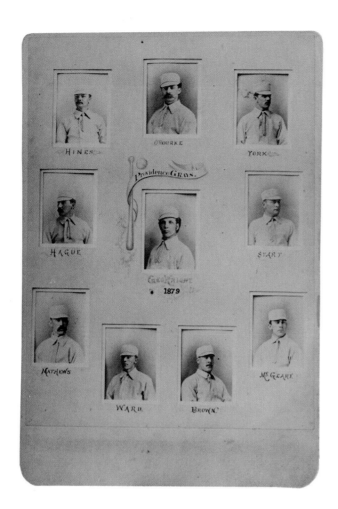

The 1879 Providence Grays. George Wright left his brother's Boston team to become player-manager of the Providence Grays. Providence won the league championship, breaking a two-year Boston streak. *From the Cooper collection.*

Fred Dunlap Union Association Batting Title Medal. 1884. *From the Cooper collection.*

Maroons, and directly compete with the American Association franchise, the St. Louis Browns. The Browns, however, not only won that battle but went on to win four consecutive American Association pennants, 1885-1888. The Browns, possibly the best team of the late 1880s, were led by Charles Comiskey. They tied Chicago for the 1885 World Series and defeated Cap Anson's Chicago Club in 1886, but lost to Detroit in 1887, and New York in 1888.

1888 St. Louis Browns. *From the Cooper collection.*

This period of growth in professional baseball, in the 1880s and early 1890s, was also a time of major growth for many of the prominent game manufacturers. As with other home games, baseball games represented an area of interest of society that was capitalized upon. Baseball games from this era are rare, with over half of them being produced by McLoughlin Brothers.

In the year 1890 the Players League was formed. The origin of the league can be traced to the control the owners took from the players when they formed the National League in 1876. It was generally perceived that the reserve clause of 1883 lowered player's salaries and limited their freedom of movement. Players were also threatened with expulsion and blackballing by the owners. In 1885 the players formed a union, or Brotherhood of Professional Baseball Players, with John Montgomery Ward, a star player and lawyer, as chief organizer. The Brotherhood was to be used for collective bargaining. In 1885, the owners formed a system of classification of players and established salary caps. Players were rated by the owners according to their ability and to their "obedience." Class A had a salary cap of $2500, Class B, $2250, Class C, $2000, Class D, $1750, and Class E, $1500. In 1890 Ward gave the owners of the National League and American Association teams an ultimatum to dissolve the reserve clause and player classification. When the owners balked, Ward formed his own league - The Players League.

This eight team league had many of the great players from both the American Association and National League, and went head to head with the National League. With teams in Pittsburgh, Chicago, New York, Philadelphia, Boston, Brooklyn, Buffalo, and Cleveland, the Player's League fielded star players like Mike Kelly, Charles Comiskey, Ned Hanlon, Roger Conner, Jim O'Rourke, Buck Ewing, Tim Keefe, Harry Stovey, Dan Brouthers, and John Montgomery Ward. With this talent it is understandable why the Player's League was successful, outdrawing the National League in its first year.

But that was not the perception. In an effort to stop the upstart league, Al Spalding, czar of the National League, falsified National League attendance figures so that the public believed that the National League outdrew the Player's League. Spalding called the Players League bluff, and many of the Players League owners and players blinked. Convinced that they had failed to overcome the National League's hold on the game, the Player's League entered into negotiations that included the American Association. Spalding proposed to the American Association that there would be a fair redistribution of the Player League players and promised no reprisals on Player League players and no salary cap. However, many

1890 Chicago White Stocking Base Ball Club of the Players League. Charles Comiskey is at the top center.

of the stars indeed ended up on National League rosters and although the American Association finished the 1891 season, it was its last. In the fall of 1891, four of the American Association clubs joined the National League to form a 12-team league - the only major league. The new teams were St. Louis, Louisville, Baltimore, and Washington. The reformed league was called the National League and American Association of Professional Baseball Clubs. The Boston, Baltimore, and Brooklyn clubs were such dominant clubs in the late 1890s, that there was a loss of public interest in the professional game. Adding to the disenchantment with baseball was a system that allowed interlocking ownership in many clubs. Owners with shares in two or more different clubs were actually able to move players to teams opportunistically to improve their standings and guarantee a pennant winner.

A New Century, A New League

In 1900 the National League returned to an 8 team league, dropping Baltimore, St. Louis, Washington and Cleveland. With the dropping of four teams, there were established baseball markets without teams and ball players without jobs. To fill the void, the Western League, a strong minor league system, was proclaimed to be the American League by its president, Ban Johnson. This occurred in 1901, with teams in Philadelphia, Boston, Baltimore, Washington, Cleveland, Detroit, St. Louis and New York. This came at a time when there was divisiveness within the National League over the naming of a new president. This allowed the American League to flourish and in 1903 a national agreement was signed which allowed the American League and National League to operate as equal but separate leagues, recognizing schedules, and player contracts.

From 1902 to 1913, the players continued to play without a voice in their future. There was no player representation in the National Commission, which controlled baseball "by its own decree...enforcing them without the aid of law and making it answerable to no one power outside its own."

The years from 1903 to approximately 1914 were known as the dead ball era. This does not refer to the ball itself (the cork centered ball was introduced in 1910), but to the style of play. Baseball was defensive, scientific style of play, with hit and run, base stealing, and bunting. Pitching dominated this era with the likes of Christy Mathewson, Grover Cleveland Alexander, Cy Young, and Walter Johnson on the mound.

In 1914 a group of wealthy entrepreneurs decided to organize their own major league, called the Federal League. Promising higher salaries and giving the players a greater say in their own destiny, teams were formed in Chicago, Baltimore, Buffalo, Pittsburgh, Indianapolis, Brooklyn, St. Louis, and Kansas City. Although the National League suffered from the competition, the Federal League could not compete. After the National League gave five million dollars in compensation to the Federal League, it was dissolved after 1915, having played two seasons.

Long ball did not come into play until approximately 1919, when Babe Ruth of the Red Sox hit 29 home runs. His timing was great for the game. 1919 was the year of the Black Sox scandal, bringing baseball to its darkest hour. Babe Ruth and the home run came to the aid of our national game, providing it with a superstar and increased popularity. Helped by the spirited attitudes of the Roaring Twenties and the national prosperity, Ruth's skill and personality led the game into its golden age.

At about the same time, in the late teens and early 1920s, many of the early game manufacturers went out of business or were sold. McLoughlin Brothers was bought by Milton Bradley. Many of the other game companies also went bankrupt as the depression approached.

The Great Depression brought an end to the golden age of baseball. Attendance dropped significantly, particularly in 1931 and 1932. Due to the financial pressures, salaries were cut. Salaries totaled $4 million dollars in 1929, but only $3 million in 1932. The effect on the teams was uneven. The wealthiest teams prospered during the period, while the poorest teams often sold their star players to the wealthier teams, such as the Yankees, Red Sox and Cubs, just to remain solvent. In the mid-1930s, with the introduction of night baseball (the first was in Cincinnati) and the broadcasting of games on radio, increased revenues improved the bottom line for many of the poor teams, helping them to endure the hard times.

With the coming of World War II, President Roosevelt urged that professional baseball continue to help keep the national spirit strong. Major league baseball was more than willing to do its part, but many of the players enlisted in the armed forces and went to war. Their places were taken by lesser players, so that it was not a particularly stellar time for professional baseball. In Chicago, Wrigley introduced the concept of women's baseball, and the league enjoyed some popularity into the 1950s.

At the end of the war the players returned, with many of them picking up their careers where they left off. It was then that Branch Rickey and Jackie Robinson made baseball history by integrating the Brooklyn Dodgers. The success of their daring experiment encouraged others to do the same, undoing nearly 100 years of racial segregation in the game.

From its beginnings the game of baseball has taken several twists and turns, but its essential timelessness is unchanged. Still it is a game of strategy and skill, a game that can continue eternally. It is a game played in parks, all alike in their neat geometries, yet each with its own idiosyncracies and personality, each with its own stories, its own myths. This same paradox of similarity and dissimilarity is reflected in the games that have found their ways into our homes over the decades. While all are alike in their basic structure, each has its own shape and attitude, its own personality and character. That is part of what makes them such a joy to collect and play.

Chapter 1

Baseball Games: Reflections of the Sport

The parallel between the growth of the sport of baseball and the development of American game companies is not exact, but there are similarities and their histories frequently coincide.

In the early years of baseball, the game evolved. Rules changed, the field changed, and the equipment used by players developed. Even today there are minor refinements to play: the designated hitter, the division of each league into three divisions, changes in the play-offs, free agency, salary caps. Though many might argue that any or all of these changes are not progress, no one can argue that they don't have an effect on the game.

Interestingly, as the real game has changed so have board games. As the manufactures strive to keep the games as up-to-date and realistic as possible, they make changes that reflect what is happening to the game as a whole. Sometimes the change is as subtle as the position of the players or the umpire on the playing board, and sometimes it involves using a whole new set of playing cards or figures to match the professionals.

For the historian of baseball this brings the excitement of historical accuracy to the study of board games. For the collector it gives one more tool in dating and valuing a game.

The following are some of the high points of change in the game of baseball and in home baseball games.

Spelling

The most subtle and probably the most helpful change in home baseball games is the spelling of the name itself, "base ball" vs. "baseball." Generally, two words were used before World War I, and one word was used after it. There are, of course, exceptions, since the decision to combine the two words was not "officially" made by some authority. But it is fairly safe to say that any game with baseball as one word was manufactured after World War I. The opposite conclusion is not quite as reliable, as some people stuck to the two word tradition much later, either out of tradition or to give the game an older feel.

Home Plate

In 1876 the rules stated that the home base should be white marble or stone. It was to be fixed in place so that its surface was flush with the surface of the ground. One corner was to face the pitcher's position, and that corner touched the intersection of the foul lines. Home plate was 12 inches square. This shape was the norm until 1900, when it was changed to the pentagon shape that we know today. The pentagonal home base was seventeen inches wide, the same width as the diagonal of the older square or diamond-shaped plate.

The earliest baseball board game, the New Parlor Game of Baseball, has the square home plate, as does every other 19th century baseball board game. Most games produced after 1900 have the pentagonal plate, but this is not a hard and fast rule. Most pre-1900 games have the diamond or four-sided home plate.

Player's Positions

In the early days of baseball, the game was played with what is called the "fair-foul rule." Prior to the mid-1880s, any ball which touched fair ground, or a person or player standing in fair territory, and then went into foul territory before passing first or third base, was considered a ball in play. Many players developed the skills to hit in this way so they could add this to their offensive repertoire. To defend against the fair-foul hit, the first and third basemen would play in foul territory.

This foul position of first and third basemen can be seen on several of the board games produced before 1890, including the 1884 Bliss game and the 1878 Parlor Base Ball Game. Games designed after 1890, show the third baseman and first baseman playing in fair territory as is seen today.

Players Bench

The players position off the field is also helpful in dating a board game. Until 1884, when the National League amended its rules to provide a player's bench for both teams, the team at bat sat on the one bench provided. The 1878 Parlor Game of Base Ball shows a single bench, and the 1884 Bliss Parlor Base Ball Game shows two benches. The 1869 New Parlor game shows no bench.

The Foul Bound

The New Parlor Game of Base Ball has an umpire's card which has play "number one" listed as a "foul bound." Prior to 1883, a foul ball caught on one bounce was considered an out. After 1883, the ball had to be caught on the fly. A similar rule, in the mid-1860s was the basis of the sheet music "Catch it on the Fly," which pertained to catching fair balls on the fly, not on the bounce, to make an out.

Bats

In the 1870s, 1880s, and early 1890s, many of the bats used were ring bats. In addition, the handle had a mushroom configuration and was thicker than today's usual bats. Ring bats seen on the cover of the game of Baseball by McLoughlin Brothers, dated 1899, shows a period type bat, as does the National League Ball Game by Yankee Novelty Co.

Player's Equipment

Though in the earliest days of baseball the game was played bare handed, gloves were used in the 1870s and 1880s to protect the player's catching hands. However, this wearing of gloves was considered to be somewhat cowardly, and up to the mid-1880s, the only player who actually wore a glove was the catcher. Games dated after the mid-1880s will show some fielders with gloves, but most definitely the catcher with a glove. The design was one initially for protection, not to aid in catching. The catcher's mask was invented in 1873 by Fred W. Thayer from Harvard, and Jim Tyng was the first person to regularly wear it. Thus, games showing the catcher's mask would obviously have to be after this date. Catcher's equipment such as the chest protector was utilized in the late 1880s and into the 1890s. Again, this is another way to help date a 19th century baseball game.

Pitching

Prior to 1884, the pitcher's position was a space 6 feet square, 45 feet from the center of home plate. "The ball must be delivered to the bat with the arms swinging nearly perpendicular at the side of the body and the hands swinging forward must pass below the hip." Thus, this was underhanded or softball-type pitching. Many of the games from this era depicted the pitcher pitching underhanded. The underhanded pitching restriction was lifted in 1884. In 1881, the pitcher's mound was move to 50 feet from home plate. It was not until 1893, that the pitching box was changed to a "rubber plate", or pitching rubber, 12 inches by 4 inches and the distance being 60 feet, 6 inches. Thus many of the early 19th century games prior to 1884 show the pitcher pitching underhanded. An example, such as the Game of Base Ball copyrighted 1886 by the McLoughlin Brothers, obviously shows the ball players playing without any benches and the pitcher pitching underhanded. This scene obviously was to depict a game taking place earlier than 1886, when the game was made.

Into the 1890s, a mound was not present, thus most 19th century games will not show a pitching mound.

Balls and Strikes.

From 1876 to 1879, every third ball delivered was considered a "ball", in other words, not in the strike zone. When "three balls" were delivered it was considered a walk. So actually, every ninth pitch out of the strike zone was a walk. In 1880, eight balls was considered a walk; in 1881 seven balls a walk; in 1884 six balls a walk. Rules changed back to seven balls in 1886. In 1887, if you were hit by a pitcher, it was a walk, and also five balls were a walk. During the 1887 season, it was the only year where four strikes was an out, rather than three strikes. In 1889 the rules changed to four balls being a walk. Thus, Baseball, the card game, which shows six balls as a walk, would be dated 1884. The Lawson's card game which shows seven balls as a walk, was actually patented in 1884 and could either be utilizing the rule from 1881 to 1884. It is extremely difficult to decide which is the first baseball card game. I feel that it is either the Lawson's game or the much more rare Base Ball card game in which six balls was considered a walk.

Condition

Games are usually comprised of the box lid (or top), the side panels (or aprons), and the box bottom which usually contains the game board and implements. The most important part of the game is usually the game box lid, the portion of the game used for display. There is no agreed upon grading system as there is in grading baseball cards.

Often, the aprons of a game are split at the corners, torn, or missing. Oftentimes this does not detract from the display-ability of the game. When assessing condition one must take into account the age of many of these games, sometimes more than 100 years, and make allowances. The following are conditions that I feel are a fair representation of games.

Mint: a game that has all the wrapping intact, has never been played with, and is obviously pristine.

Near mint: a game that has been played with but has no discoloration or markings.

Excellent: these may have mild imperfections and wear, but the print on the game box and board is clean. There may be minor splitting of the box apron corners, along with damage to the aprons. A lid of a box that is missing less than 20% of one of the aprons could still be considered an excellent game if the game top meets the other criteria.

Very good: colors may be faded, the implements worn, and at least two of the apron corners split. Loss of 20-40% of one and possibly two aprons, or tears in the aprons. Less than 5% loss of the box top image would also fit into this category.

Good: tears or discoloration and up to 10% of the lithography or box cover showing damage. Loss or splitting of three of the apron corners with sometimes loss of greater than 50% of one or two aprons.

Fair: heavy usage is evident, with all the apron corners split and possibly missing more than 50% of all the aprons. Holes or loss of the box lid, if it does not seriously impact the display-ability.

Poor: warped or crushed box. All the aprons torn or missing. A significant amount of the lithography or printing of the box lid missing.

Chapter 2

The First Base Ball Games

From the Cooper collection

Although the first baseball game produced has never been definitively documented, two games seem to vie for the title: "Base-Ball Table" by William Buckley of New York, New York, and "Parlor Base Ball" by Francis C. Sebring of Hoboken, New Jersey.

Mr. Sebring, a pitcher for the Empire Base Ball Club of New York, was apparently the first to have the idea for a game to be used by an invalid base ball player. Patent papers for Sebring's game are dated February 8, 1868 and Buckley's patent paper are dated August 20, 1867. However, an advertisement for Sebring's Parlor Base Game appears in the December 8, 1866 issue of *Frank Leslie's Illustrated Newspaper*.

Sebring's Parlor Base Ball Game is approximately two feet wide. What is ironic is that it is the shape of a pentagon, which was not utilized as home plate until 1900. A coin is placed in the pitching slot and is propelled forward by a spring mechanism. A bat strikes the coin which can slide into holes at the positions of fielders, putting the batter out, or fall into the field as a base hit. Any wooden device for runners, such as a pawn, can be used. If the batted coin hits a runner, he is considered out. The pitcher acts as an infielder and when the coin is caught by him, it can be shot to any base for a force out. The retail price for the game in 1866 was $5, a significant amount for the time. It could also be obtained by organizing a group of people to buy seven subscriptions of *Frank Leslie's Boys and Girls Weekly* at $2.50 each.

Buckley's Base Ball Table shows a ball pitched along a groove to the batter. A second home plate is used for the runner, reminiscent of the Massachusetts Game. He advances to each base through grooves in the board. The bases are hollowed out to allow the ball to fall into them. A hit ball may be caught by metal clasps at the fielder's positions. A mace or cue is used to push the hit ball to the base to "tag" out the runner. Metal straps traverse the bases and a second ball acts as a runner.

The earliest known base ball game to exist is the New Parlor Game of Base Ball, by N.B. Sumner, 1869.

Patent drawings for William Buckley's baseball Game Board, granted on August 20, 1867.

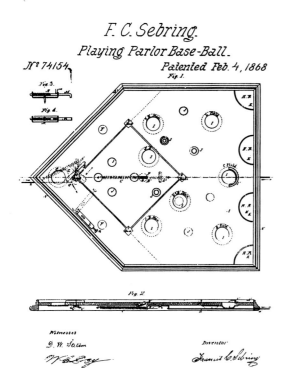

F. C. Sebring.
Playing Parlor Base-Ball.
Nº 74154
Patented Feb. 4, 1868

This illustration from "Frank Leslie's Illustrated Newspaper," December 8, 1866 accompanies an article describing Sebring's game. It calls it "the most attractive parlor game in vogue, and one in every way calculated to instruct ladies, youth, and amateur ball players in the theory of the "national game."

Patent drawings for Francis C. Sebring's Parlor Base-Ball game, dated February 4, 1868.

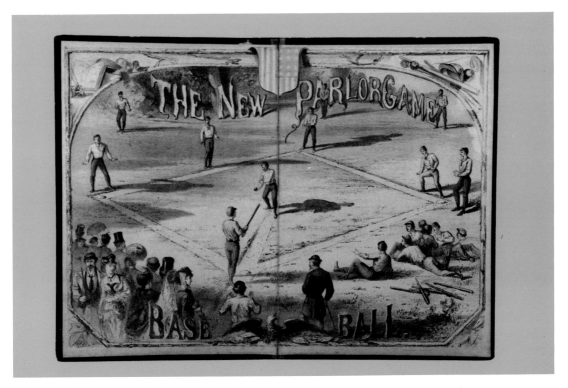

The New Parlor Game of Base Ball, 1869. There are several point of interest. The pitcher is tossing underhanded, most likely 45 feet from home plate. The first and third basemen are ready to cover foul territory due to the fair foul rule, which stated that a ball which touched in fair territory but went foul before reaching first or third base remained in play. There is no players' bench, because it was not mandated until the 1870s. Fielders are barehanded and dressed in the bib uniforms of the era. Home plate is not in a diamond shape. There are women present at this gentlemanly game. *From the Cooper collection.*

The complete game includes the game board, an accessory box, and a spinner with a bat and the numbers 1-30. The choices include out on a foul bound, because, prior to 1883, a foul ball caught on a bounce was an out. Another choice, number 6, "three called balls take a base," referred to a rule that stated that three pitches that were not strikes were considered one ball, and three of these balls were a walk. This rule was changed in 1881. The player, of course, called his own pitches. The game also includes rules for playing, an umpire card, playing pieces, and score cards with blanks spaces to create one's own team. In addition there are pre-printed score cards with the players for teams made up of actual line-ups and some "picked teams" drawing players from various teams. A roster of a "dozen leading base ball nines of America," Red Stockings, Haymakers, Atlantic, Athletic, Lowell, Eckfords, Harvards, Forest City, Stars, Mutual, Tri-Mountains, and Fairmounts, lists players from each of these teams. N.B. Sumner. 17.25" x 12.25". *From the Cooper collection.*

The Umpire card with the results of various spins.

THE NEW PARLOR GAME
OF
BASE BALL.
UMPIRE.

1. Out on a foul bound, ...
2. A long hit to centre field, . . . One base
3. A hot grounder to short stop, . Out at first base
4. A clean home run. . . . .
5. A sky-scraper to left field, . . Out on the fly
6. Three called balls, ... One base
7. A liner to centre field, . . . Out on the fly
8. Out on the fly by first base. . . .
9. A daisy cutter to right field, . . Two bases
10. A sharp grounder to third base, Out at first base
11. A corker to left field, . . . Three bases
12. A fly to center field—muffed, . . One base
13. A hot liner to second base, . . . Out
14. A safe hit over short stop, . . One base
15. A base on a balk. . . . .
16. Out on a foul fly. . . . .
17. Three strikes missed by a catcher, . One base
18. A safe hit to left field, . . . One base
19. A clean home run. . . . .
20. An easy fly to pitcher—muffed, . . One base
21. Three strikes, ... Out
22. A fly to right field—muffed, . . One base
23. A fly to short stop, ... Out
24. A fly to right field, ... Out
25. A safe one over second base, . . One Base
26. A red hot grounder to 3rd base, sent to 1st base, Out
27. A clean home run. . . . .
28. A hot liner (perfect beauty) to pitcher, Out on the fly
29. A long hit to centre field . . . Two bases
30. A long foul hit to left field, . Out on the bound

Chapter 3

19th Century Player-Endorsed Games

These are the rarest of games, with only three pictorial endorsed games known to exist, the Zimmer's Base Ball Game, The Champion Game of Base Ball, and The World's Game of Base Ball. As base ball evolved through its silver and golden eras, the use of players' names to endorse games became more prevalent.

Zimmer's Base Ball Game. The beauty of the game lies in the chromolithographic depiction of eighteen major league players. The likeness is incredible.

The players in the field are Buck Ewing, catcher (Hall of Fame), Amos Rusie, pitcher (Hall of Fame), Dan Brouthers, first base (Hall of Fame), John Montgomery Ward, second base (Hall of Fame), John Glasscock, shortstop (Cleveland), George Stacey Davis, third base (Cleveland), Billy Hamilton, left (Hall of Fame), Jimmy McAleer, center (Cleveland), Sam Thompson, right (Hall of Fame).

Portraits in the dugout are Cy Young (Hall of Fame), Kid Nichols (Hall of Fame), W. Zimmer (not known, perhaps a relative of the game maker), Jacob Virtue (Cleveland), Bud McPhee (Cincinnati), George Davies (Cleveland), Patsy Tebeau (Cleveland), Ed Delahanty (Hall of Fame), Germany Smith (Cincinnati). Louis Charles "Chief" Zimmer, an accomplished catcher, is pictured in front of home plate. His claim to fame is being the first catcher to play close to home plate and to routinely throw out runners stealing. McLoughlin, 20" x 20".

This game is the Mona Lisa of all baseball games. It is the most valuable, beautiful, and desired game. It is an enigma why Chief Zimmer was chosen to be responsible for producing this masterpiece, but he certainly remembered to include many of his Cleveland team mates. *From the Cooper collection.*

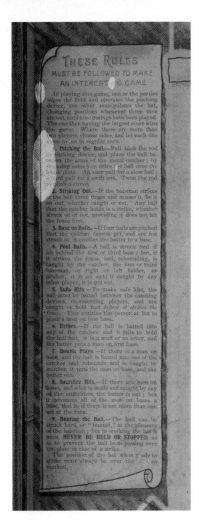

Chief Zimmer
Games: 1280
At bats: 4546
Hits: 1224
Home runs: 26
Runs: 617
RBIs: 620
Batting Avg.: .269

Germany Smith
Games: 1710
At bats: 6552
Hits: 1592
Home runs: 45
Runs: 907
RBIs: 618
Batting Avg.: .243

Ed Delahanty
Games: 1835
At bats: 7509
Hits: 2597
Home runs: 100
Runs: 1601
RBIs: 1464
Batting Avg.: .346
Hall of Fame: 1945

Patsy Tebeau
Games: 1167
At bats: 4618
Hits: 1291
Home runs: 27
Runs: 671
RBIs: 735
Batting Avg.: .280

Dan Brouthers
Games: 1673
At bats: 6711
Hits: 2296
Home runs: 106
Runs: 1523
RBIs: 1057
Batting Avg.: .342
Hall of Fame: 1945

George Stacey Davis
Games: 2376
At bats: 9050
Hits: 2667
Home runs: 74
Runs: 1544
RBIs: 1435
Batting Avg.: .295

Buck Ewing
Games: 1315
At bats: 5363
Hits: 1625
Home runs: 70
Runs: 1129
RBIs: 738
Batting Avg.: .303
Hall of Fame: 1939

Billy Hamilton
Games: 1593
At bats: 6284
Hits: 2163
Home runs: 40
Runs: 1692
RBIs: 736
Batting Avg.: .344
Hall of Fame: 1961

DAVIES. McPHEE. VIRTUE. W. ZIMMER. NICHOLS. YOUNG.

George Davies
Games: 46
Wins: 18
Losses: 24
Pct.: .429
ERA: 3.32

Bid McPhee
Games: 2137
At bats: 8301
Hits: 2260
Home runs: 52
Runs: 1684
RBIs: 727
Batting Avg.: .272

Jake Virtue
Games: 474
At bats: 174
Hits: 483
Home runs: 7
Runs: 321
RBIs: 256
Batting Avg.: .274

Kid Nichols
Games: 620
Wins: 361
Losses: 208
Pct.: .634
ERA: 2.94
Hall of Fame: 1949

Cy Young
Games: 906
Wins: 511
Losses: 315
Pct.: .619
ERA: 2.63
Hall of Fame: 1937

Jack Glasscock
Games: 1736
At bats: 7030
Hits: 2040
Home runs: 27
Runs: 1163
RBIs: 779
Batting Avg.: .290

Jimmy McAleer
Games: 1020
At bats: 3977
Hits: 1006
Home runs: 13
Runs: 619
RBIs: 469
Batting Avg.: .253

Amos Rusie
Games: 462
Wins: 246
Losses: 174
Pct.: .586
ERA: 3.07
Hall of Fame: 1977

Sam Thompson
Games: 1410
At bats: 6005
Hits: 1986
Home runs: 128
Runs: 1263
RBIs: 1299
Batting Avg.: .331
Hall of Fame: 1974

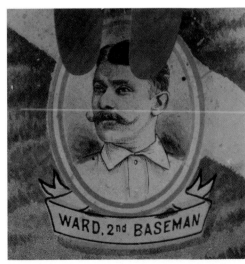

Monte Ward
Games: 1825
At bats: 7647
Hits: 2105
Home runs: 26
Runs: 1408
RBIs: 686
Batting Avg.: .275
Hall of Fame: 1964

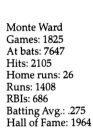

The box top of Zimmer's Base Ball Game.

No. 484—ZIMMER'S BASE BALL GAME.

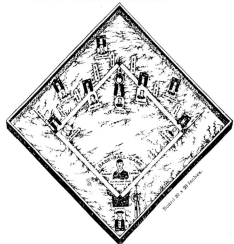

A Perfect Parlor Parallel of the Field Game.

Balls can be Pitched, Batted, and Caught. Can Pitch Swift, Slow, and Curved Balls.

A REAL BAT is used to strike at a REAL BALL PITCHED to the striker. Curved balls may be pitched. A "catcher" stands behind the bat and really catches all balls passing the striker. Should the batsman strike the ball, it will be caught by some of the "catchers" located on bases or in the field, or will pass between them if not near enough to be caught by a player in a field game. Thus, base hits, fouls, etc. are made in the regular way, and the striker and base runners are put "out" just as in the field base ball. A score with all the points of a real game may be kept. Every detail of the game is perfect.

The board, beautifully printed in colors, represents a base ball field. The "catchers" are nickel plated. The box is leatherette, stamped in gold.

Advertisement for Zimmer's Base Ball Game from McLoughlin Brothers 1895 catalog. *Courtesy of Patrice McFarland.*

ZIMMER'S BASE BALL GAME.

Balls pitched, batted and caught! Can pitch swift and slow balls! Can pitch in and out shoots.

An opportunity for enthusiasts on the subject of the National Game to enjoy something of the excitement of an actual base ball game in their homes, is found in this miniature affair, in which the ball is pitched and batted and, if not hit safely, is instantly caught out as in the regular out-door game.

The diagram of the ball field is 22 inches square, and all the players' positions are filled with spring catches fastened to the board; these serve to stop and hold the ball, seldom failing to hold a "hot one" direct from the bat, and the chances for a safe hit are found to be about the same as in an actual game between professional nines.

Price, per dozen $8.00

Advertisement for the Zimmer game as it appeared in the Carl P. Stirn company catalog of New York. *Courtesy of Patrice McFarland.*

C. Zimmer, Old Judge card. *From the Cooper collection.*

Charles Comiskey
Games: 1390
At bats: 5796
Hits: 1531
Home runs: 29
Runs: 994
RBIs: 467
Batting Avg.: .264
Hall of Fame: 1939

Bob Ferguson
Games: 562
At bats: 2306
Hits: 625
Home runs: 1
Runs: 346
RBIs: 200
Batting Avg.: .271

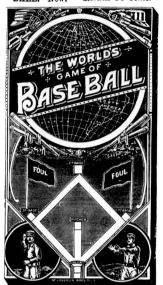

No. 550—WORLD'S GAME OF BASE BALL. New. *Retails 50 Cents.*

The *World's Game of Base Ball* is a new and very complete game, affording in the parlor or home the closest counterpart of a genuine Base Ball game that has yet been produced. It is gotten up in very elegant style, making it one of the most showy and desirable games we have ever offered at the price. It sells at sight.

The World's Game of Base Ball. The significance of this game is that it is the only McLoughlin game to commemorate an historical baseball event. In 1889, when the game was produced, an all-star team of major leaguers toured the world to introduce the game abroad. The two players depicted are Charles Comiskey and Robert Ferguson. 16" x 9". *From the Cooper collection.*

The advertisement for The World's Game of Base Ball as it appeared in the McLoughlin Brother's Catalog. As it says, "It is gotten up in very elegant style, making it one of the most showy and desirable games we have ever offered at the price. It sells at sight."

The rules on the inside box top of The World's Game of Base Ball, along with some of the nicely turned wooden playing pieces. *From the Cooper collection.*

Round album photo of Comiskey. *From the Cooper collection.*

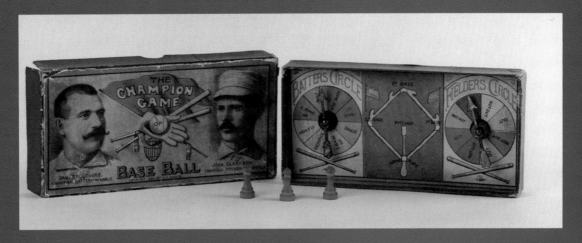

Dan Brouthers
Games: 1673
At bats: 6711
Hits: 2296
Home runs: 106
Runs: 1523
RBIs: 1057
Batting Avg.: .342
Hall of Fame: 1945

John Clarkson
Games: 531
Wins: 326
Losses: 177
Pct.: .648
ERA: 2.81
Hall of Fame: 1963

The Champion Game of Base Ball, 1889. This double spinner game is exceedingly rare and it is one of the three player endorsed games from the 19th century. Pictured is Dan Brouthers, Champion Batter of the World, and John Clarkson, Champion Pitcher of the World. A.S. Schutz. 7.5" x 3.5". *From the Cooper collection.*

Cap Anson
Games: 2276
At bats: 9108
Hits: 3000
Home runs: 96
Runs: 1719
RBIs: 1715
Batting Avg.: .329
Hall of Fame: 1939

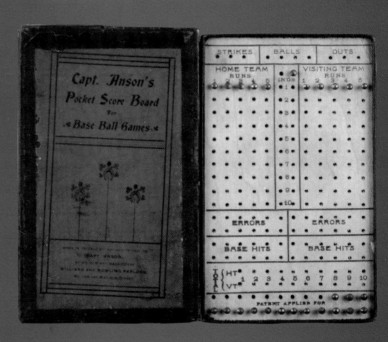

Captain Anson's Pocket Score Board for Base Ball Games, 1897. Although not truly a game itself, this is a scoreboard used to keep score at games. Its importance is that Cap Anson was probably the most significant player of the 19th century, and the first player to accumulate 3000 hits. 7" x 4.5". *From the Cooper collection.*

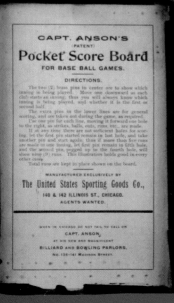

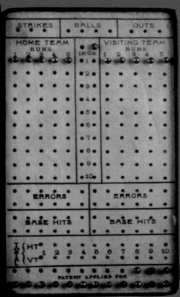

On the inside of the lid of the Pocket Score Board is an advertisement for Anson's billiards parlor in Chicago. *From the Cooper collection.*

King Kelly
Games: 1455
At bats: 5894
Hits: 1813
Home runs: 69
Runs: 1357
RBIs: 793
Batting Avg.: .308
Hall of Fame: 1945

Tim Keefe
Games: 600
Wins: 342
Losses: 225
Pct.: .603
ERA: 2.62
Hall of Fame: 1964

19th Century Bowling Pins. While not technically player endorsed, the player decals on this group of six bowling pins are images of Cap Anson, Tim Keefe, Mike "King" Kelly, John Montgomery Ward, Buck Ewing, and Charles Comiskey. Manufacturer unknown. 8" high. *From the Cooper collection.*

Chapter 4

19th Century Non-Endorsed Games

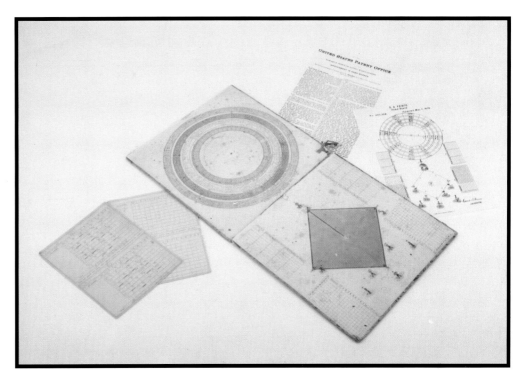

Parlor Base Ball, 1878. This is the actual production version of the game. Note the location of the first and third basemen, actually playing in foul territory. At this time in baseball, a ball which touched fair but went foul before reaching first or third was considered to be in play. Therefore the first and third basemen had to play the foul ball and situate themselves in foul territory. Also note the location of the catcher, umpire with umbrella, and a single players' bench. E.B. Peirce. 10" x 10" closed. *From the Cooper collection.*

This prototype of 1878 Parlor Baseball game was actually submitted with the patent application. Shown with it are a copy of patent application and score cards from the final version of the game. When it went into production, some of details were changed. *From the Cooper collection.*

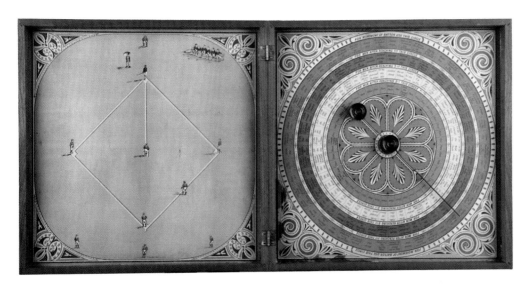

The outside of the Parlor Base Ball game. *From the Cooper collection.*

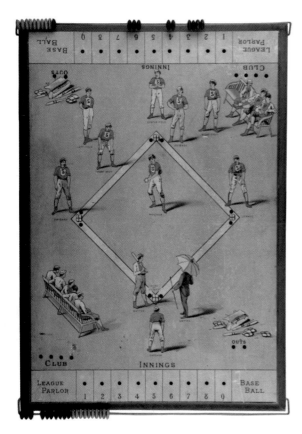

LEAGUE PARLOR BASE BALL.

NEW AND NOVEL.

A GAME THAT CAN BE PLAYED AROUND THE EVENING LAMP.

The R. Bliss Manufacturing Co. Catalogue of 1889 shows the New Parlor Base Ball Game, though it calls it "League Parlor Base Ball." *Courtesy of Patrice McFarland.*

The New Parlor Game of Base Ball, 1884. This dice game's beauty is the chromolithography on wood. On this version the umpire has an umbrella. The game is illustrated in advertisements of the era. The first and third basemen are in position for the existing fair-foul rule. Manufactured by Bliss. 15" x 11". *From the Cooper collection.*

The New Parlor Game of Base Ball, 1884. Similar to the previous example except that the umpire has no umbrella and is taking notes, and there is two benches instead of one. Bliss, 15" x 11". *From the Cooper collection.*

S.D. Hadley & Company New Base Ball Game, 1885. A teetotum (spinner-top) game. The number of the teetotum touching the ground determines an out, single, double, triple, or home run. Hadley & Co. was a Boston shoe manufactrer, and this game was an advertising give-away. "While playing this game remember that S.D. Hadley & Co. give it away to every boy or girl who purchases a pair of boots or shoes at either of their stores." Copyrighted by H.H. Durgin. 4" x 4".*From the Cooper collection.*

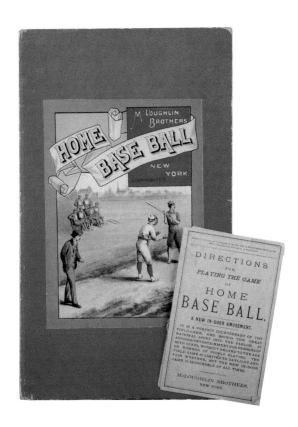

The front of the 1886 Home Base Ball game, with directions. *From the Cooper collection.*

Home Base Ball, 1886. This game was unboxed and sold with the directions and the game board only. It utilized two standard dice. The combinations from 2-12 dictated the play. The beautiful graphics have the New York skyline in the background. McLoughlin. 15.5" x 13" open. *From the Cooper collection.*

Base Ball, 1886. A spinner game. J.H. Singer, New York. *From the Cooper collection.*

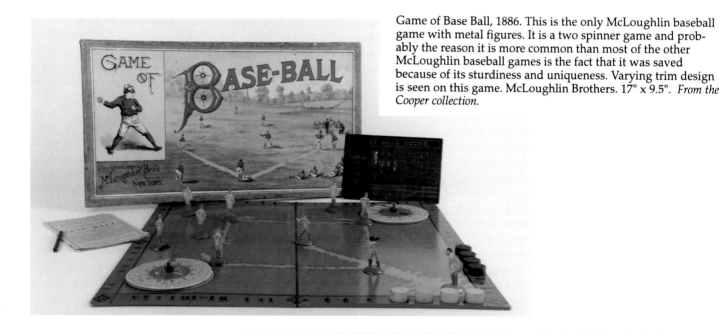

Game of Base Ball, 1886. This is the only McLoughlin baseball game with metal figures. It is a two spinner game and probably the reason it is more common than most of the other McLoughlin baseball games is the fact that it was saved because of its sturdiness and uniqueness. Varying trim design is seen on this game. McLoughlin Brothers. 17" x 9.5". *From the Cooper collection.*

The back side of the Game of Base Ball is an attractive design. *From the Cooper collection.*

34

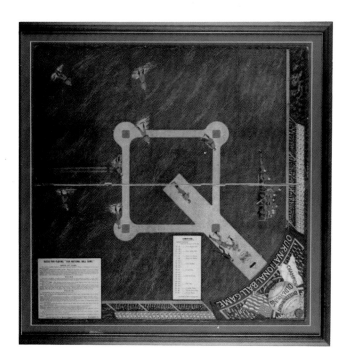

Our National Ball Game, 1887. A two-dice game. This version has the Spalding logo behind home plate. Printed by E.I. Hoag, another version (1886) has the initials E.I.H. in the diamond behind home plate. They have been blotted out in this version. McGill and Delany, Philadelphia. *From the Cooper collection.*

McGILL & DELANY'S
OUR NATIONAL BALL GAME
(PLAYED WITH 2 DICE AND 9 COUNTERS.)

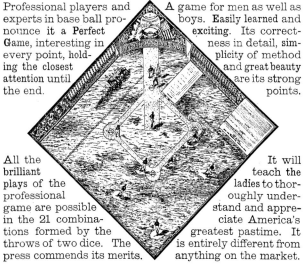

Professional players and experts in base ball pronounce it a **Perfect Game**, interesting in every point, holding the closest attention until the end.

A game for men as well as boys. Easily learned and exciting. Its correctness in detail, simplicity of method and great beauty are its strong points.

All the brilliant plays of the professional game are possible in the 21 combinations formed by the throws of two dice. The press commends its merits.

It will teach the ladies to thoroughly understand and appreciate America's greatest pastime. It is entirely different from anything on the market.

"**OUR NATIONAL BALL GAME**" is a revolution in indoor amusements. Two to eighteen persons can play, forming two sides; the throws of the dice indicating flies, fouls, strikes, balls, hits, errors, double-plays, home-runs, etc., all proportionally arranged, thus: 1-2, a base hit; 2-3, a strike; 2-6, a foul, etc., a small counter being placed to represent a player's position on base.

The annexed score shows a game played on this principle, and demonstrates at once its close similarity to the official game:

Innings,	1	2	3	4	5	6	7	8	9	Runs	Base Hits	Errors
Gentlemen	0	1	2	2	0	0	0	2	0	7	11	3
Ladies	0	1	1	4	0	0	0	0	0	6	8	5

"**OUR NATIONAL BALL GAME**" is a folding game, 18 x 18; the above cut showing but partly its great beauty. It is printed in six colors, highly ornamented, and its appearance in the window attracts much attention. Each game includes a dice-cup, dice and counters.

An advertisement for Our National Ball Game, as it appeared in the A.J. Reach & Co.'s Catalogue. A.J. Reach was a prominent sporting goods house in Philadelphia. *Courtesy of Barry Sloate.*

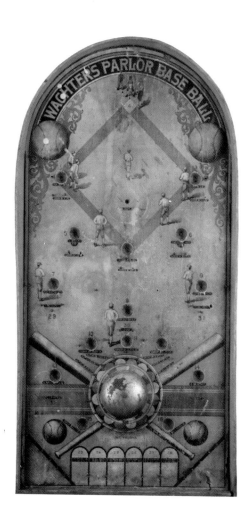

Wachter's Parlor Base Ball, 1888. A bagatelle game missing its shooter at the pitcher's position. The hole the ball falls into determines the outcome of the play. Wachter. Wood and paper, 25" x 12". *From the Cooper collection.*

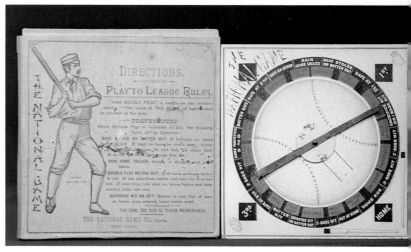

The Parlor Base Ball Game (known in the hobby as "Bostons vs. Chicagos"), 1888. A three-in-one game. The ball falls in a slot which determines play. If you open up the fortune teller box it tells your fortune and asks you an addition problem. Manufacturer unknown. Wooden case. 13" x 10.5" closed. *From the Cooper collection.*

The National Game, 1889. The square envelop front lid depicts a player of the era with directions. The reverse has a score card and the date. The game has a heavy cardboard square with a spinner. Baseball paraphernalia is lithographed at the corners. The National Game Co., New York. 5" x 5". *Courtesy of Marty and Debby Krim.*

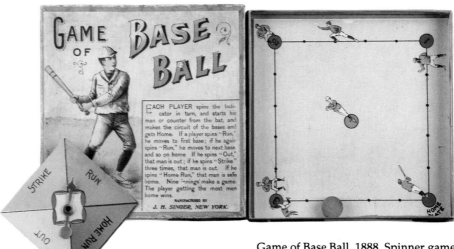

Game of Base Ball, 1888. Spinner game, featuring a typical 19th century bat with rings and a diamond shaped home plate on the cover. J.H. Singer, New York. 5" x 5". *From the Cooper collection.*

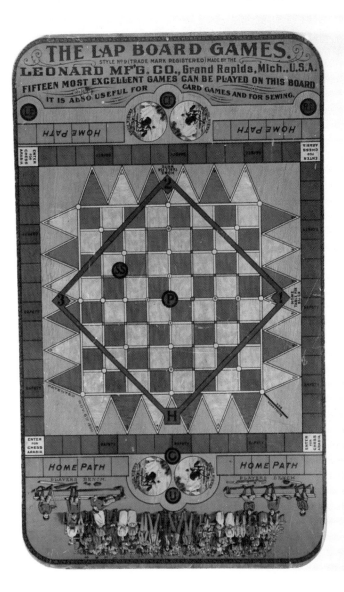

Nash Bagatelle Game, 1889. Paper on wood with bells at the top and the bottom. The final location of the ball sets the play. This one is missing the shooter. Nash Manufacturing. 20" x 9". *From the Cooper collection.*

The Lap Board Game, c. 1900. This multi-use board is paint on wood and can be used for several games including baseball, or as a portable sewing table. Leonard Manufacturing, Grand Rapids, Michigan. 18" x 30". *From the Cooper collection.*

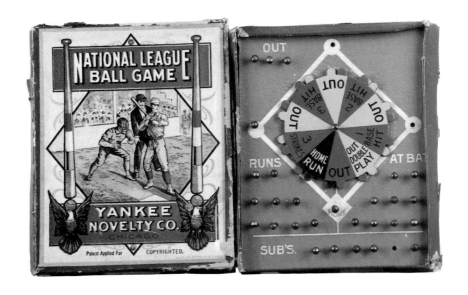

National League Ball Game, 1890. Game with metal spinner. The box top has a nice depiction of period bats and a patriotic feel. Yankee Novelty Co. 5" x 5". *From the Cooper collection.*

37

Uncle Sam's Base Ball, 1890. This is a crossover game utilizing the patriotism of Uncle Sam and the national game of baseball. The die has 14 sides, each with a symbol that determines the play. There is a scorecard with numbered squares for keeping track of the score. J.C. Bell, Cleveland, Ohio. 4.5" x 9". *From the Cooper collection.*

The Game of Parlor Base Ball, 1892. McLoughlin.18" x 20". *Courtesy of Roy and Grace Olsen.*

Base Ball Game, 1892. A McLoughlin spinner game, this looks more like the modern game. The pitcher is throwing overhand and there are two benches. The umpire still stands to the side of the catcher. On the box top we can see that the catcher's equipment includes face and chest protection. McLoughlin Brothers. 7.5" x 7.5". *From the Cooper collection.*

Mayo Cut Plug advertising game, 1893. A player figure was in every pack of Mayo Tobacco. The tobacco store would provide the playing field, or you could send fifty empty packs to Mayo and they would mail it to you. The players are from Boston and New York. It comes with a teetotum to determine the play. Mayo Tobacco Co. 8" x 16". *From the Cooper collection.*

Close-up of a player from the Mayo game. *From the Cooper collection.*

The Diamond Game of Base Ball, 1894. The rules and board of the McLoughlin spinner game. McLoughlin. 8.5" x 4". *From the Cooper collection.*

The box top of the Diamond Game of Base Ball. *From the Cooper collection.*

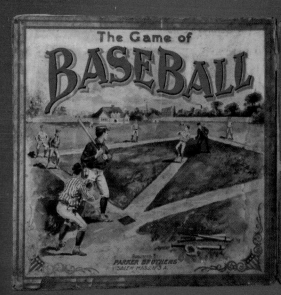

The Game of Base Ball, 1894. A dice game where the result of the roll determines the play. Parker Brothers. 15" x 15". *From the Cooper collection.*

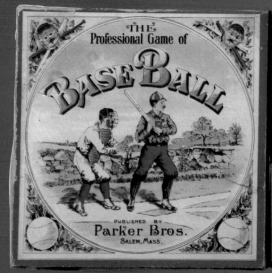

The Professional Game of Base Ball, 1896. Dice game with the throw determining the play. Parker Brothers, 8.5" x 8.5". *From the Cooper collection.*

Home Base Ball Game, 1897. This is a typical spinner-type McLoughlin game with the omnipresent batter and catcher that they used on many of their games. At later dates the sharpness of the images diminishes, because the stone used in the chromolithography process wears. McLoughlin. 20" x 10.5". *From the Cooper collection.*

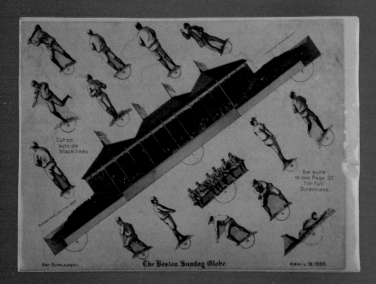

Boston Sunday Globe die cut player game, 1896. *From the Cooper collection.*

Base Ball Game, 1897. A later edition of McLoughlin's Base Ball
Game of 1892. McLoughlin spinner game. McLoughlin
Brothers. 7.5" x 7.5". *From the Cooper collection.*

The College Base Ball Game, 1898. A dice game with the
combination from 2-12 determining the outcome of the play.
This is unusual in the mentioning of college and in the
presence of women. Professional games were rough places for
women, but in college it seemed to be a bit more civilized.
Parker Brothers. 21" x 11". *From the Cooper collection.*

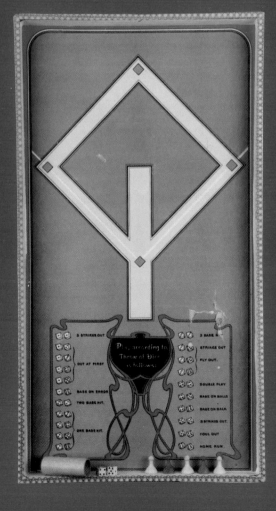

Art Nouveau graphics decorate a rather plain playing board of
the College Base Ball Game. *From the Cooper collection.*

41

The Game of Base Ball, 1899. This is an unusual five spinner game. On the box top you can see the diamond shape of home plate. It became a pentagon in 1900. You should also note the catcher's mask, the gloves the players wear, and the overhand pitching style. These all help to date a board game. McLoughlin. 22" x 13". *From the Cooper collection.*

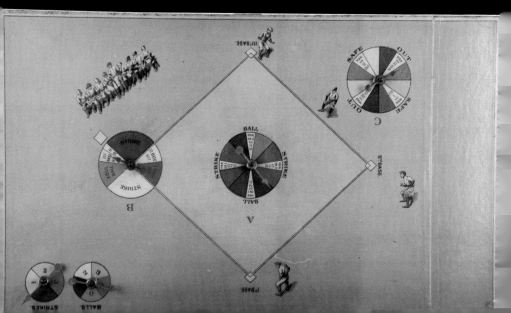

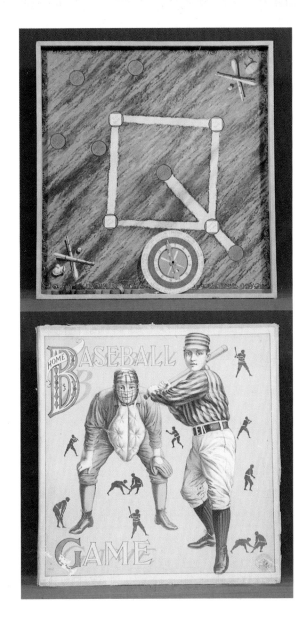

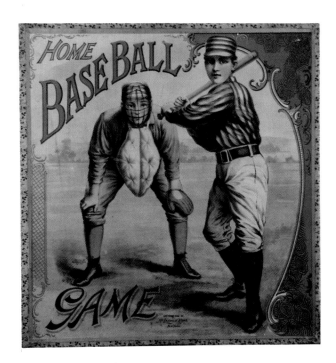

Home Base Ball Game, 1900. The same image is on this new version of the McLoughlin game. McLoughlin. 13" x 14.5". *From the Cooper collection.*

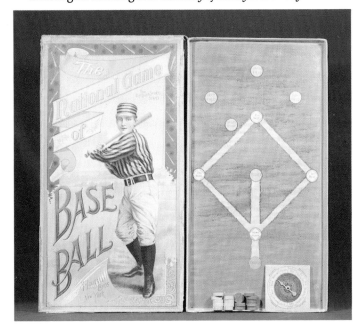

Home Base Ball, c. 1900. Number 5195 of McLoughlin. The same batter and catcher appear as on the other games, but in the background are silhouettes of baseball players in various action poses. The playing field and pieces are essentially unchanged. McLoughlin. *Courtesy of Marty and Debby Krim.*

The board of the Home Base Ball Game, 1900. *From the Cooper collection.*

The National Game of Base Ball, c. 1901. This is part of McLoughlin's "Outdoor Sports Series" of board games. The batter is the same as that used on various Home Base Ball Games, and the play of the game is the same. 11" x 20". *Courtesy of Marty and Debby Krim.*

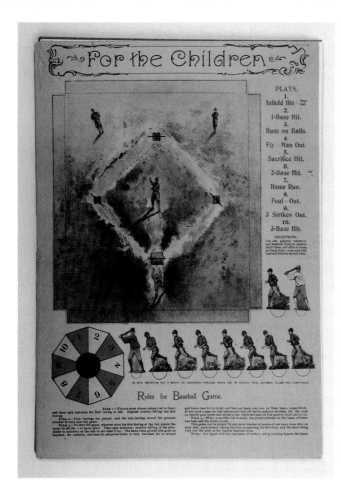

Minneapolis Times die cut baseball game, with teetotum. 1900. *From the Cooper collection.*

Thomas Base Ball Game, 1893. Each player plays from an end of the game. They propel a checker and where it lands determines the outcome. Wood and paper. 30" x 20". Paper and wood. *From the Cooper collection.*

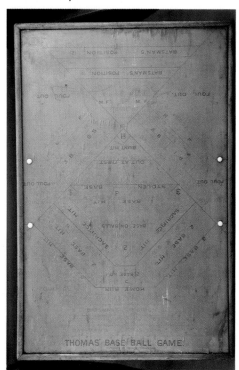

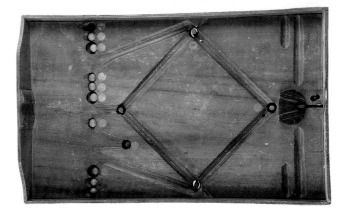

Name unknown. A spring driven bagatelle-type baseball game. Manufacturer unknown. 23.5" x 14.5". *From the Cooper collection.*

Chicago Game Series Base Ball, late 1800s. Beautifully lithographed color cover with scenes of board games, Columbia, war, and baseball. The playing field in the bottom of the box is generic. Instructions are inside the lid and on the playing field. The roll of the dice determines play. Geo. B. Doan & Co., 300 Wabash Avenue, Chicago. 18" x 18" *Courtesy of Marty and Debby Krim.*

Base Ball Dominoes, turn of century. The 2" x 7" lithographed box top features a generic player of the era. Inside are 28 wooden lithographed dominoes. Each has an action and a position. No instructions are with the game. *Courtesy of Marty and Debby Krim.*

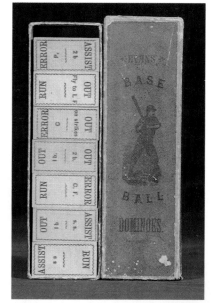

Chapter 5
19th Century Card Games

Lawson's Patent Base Ball Playing Cards, 1884. There are two versions of the this game. One is in a slide box with brown backed, gilt edged cards. The other comes in a cardboard box and has blue backed, non-gilt edged cards. The slide box set is much more rare, and when new cost twice as much as the other set. They come with 36 cards, 9 strikers, 9 plays with red corners, and 18 perfecting plays with blue corners. It also has an instruction booklet and a "value" card. Seven balls are a walk, which was the rule for the years 1881 and 1886. T.H. Lawson & Co., Boston, Massachusetts. 2.5" x 4".

Preston Orem in the book, *Baseball 1845-1881: A Supplement*, writes about the Lawson game. He notes the popularity of the game and that only one rival "took the field," J.S. Aydelott of Xenia, Ohio, who patented and put upon the market a game known as "Parlor Base Ball," played with 125 cards "representing all the features of base ball." (*see p. 116*).

Lawson, notes Orem, organized tournaments, including one with players from the National League clubs. Prizes were offered to the winning team. The teams traveled from city to city to take part in the games. Orem tells of a particular contest between St. Louis and the Chicago White Stockings, who vied for the right to meet Philadelphia in the final. A newspaper of the day gave this account of the match:

"The St. Louis men played a strong game but more familiarity with the cards was shown in the play of the Chicago hands. Luck was also on the wrong side as the cards seemed to run against the local players. A goodly number of friends of both clubs were present to witness the novel contest and all became 'cranks.' Each one learned the game in a few minutes and could explain it in a few seconds. Good card players say, however, there is fully as much science as in whist. At the finish the umpire Bowman, representing the managers of the tournament, presented winner with $40 and losers with $10.

"Williams and Pfeffer played for Chicago; Glasscock and McKinnon for St. Louis. The following is the score by innings:

| Chicago | 1 | 0 | 3 | 5 | 5 | 1 | 0 | 5 | 1 | 21 |
| St. Louis | 0 | 3 | 0 | 0 | 0 | 0 | 1 | 0 | 0 | 4 |

"As the game included 36 cards, four of which were played on each trick, there were nine tricks to each inning, and runs were scored by the difference in tricks taken. Thus one run would represent five tricks of nine; five runs, seven tricks of nine.

"Pfeffer was considered a whist expert and Williamson was a crack player of faro and most all other card games, so the Maroons were perhaps a bit overmatched." *Courtesy of Barry Sloate.*

Base Ball, 1884. This 49 card game has a playing field on the bottom of the box that shows the first and third basemen located in foul territory because of the fair-foul rule. It is also referred to as Parlor Base Ball as are most of the 19th century games. What is most significant about this game is that six balls were a walk, which was only the rule during the 1884 season. Manufacturer unknown. 5" x 6". *From the Cooper collection.*

Egerton R. Williams Base Ball, 1886. Consists of 19 cards with two four color portraits of the stars of the 1880s. These cards designate different plays, with the home run card portraying Anson and Ewing. In addition there are 36 situational cards with no portraits. The game comes with a game box, discs, and game board. The Hatch Co., New York. 3" x 5". *From the Cooper collection.*

Directions for the Williams' game. *From the Cooper collection.*

WG1, 1888. Playing cards from a deck of 72, with full-body portraits of professional players of the era. In the upper left hand corner is the team initial and the position's abbreviation over its number. In the upper right hand corner is the playing card the card represents, which also corresponds to their position. The position number is in an inverse relationship with the value of the card. Ace=position 1 (catcher), king=2 (pitcher), queen=3 (short stop), jack=4 (first base), etc. There are no cards valued 2, 3, 4, or 5 because there are only 9 people in the batting order. The rules of the game are unknown as is the manufacturer. Card size 2.5" x 3.5". *From the Cooper collection.*

Chapter 6

20th Century Player-Endorsed Games

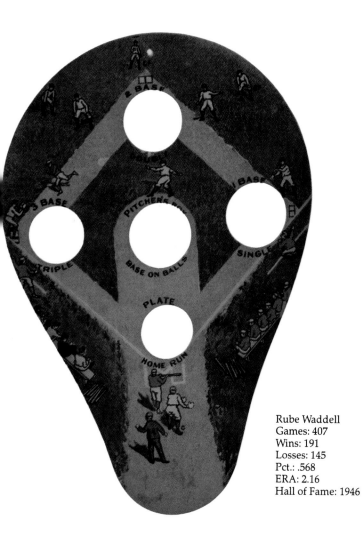

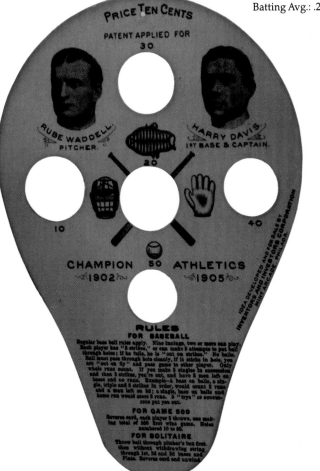

Harry Davis
Games: 1754
At bats: 6648
Hits: 1839
Home runs: 74
Runs: 998
RBIs: 951
Batting Avg.: .277

Rube Waddell
Games: 407
Wins: 191
Losses: 145
Pct.: .568
ERA: 2.16
Hall of Fame: 1946

Rube Waddell-Harry Davis Game, 1905. A ball and string were attached to the front edge of this cardboard paddle. the ball was flipped to land in one of the holes. On the front was a simple baseball game, and on the back was a scoring game Inventors and Investors Corp., Philadelphia. 6" x 4". *From the Cooper collection.*

Frank Chance
Games: 1286
At bats: 4293
Hits: 1271
Home runs: 20
Runs: 798
RBIs: 596
Batting Avg.: .296
Hall of Fame: 1946

Ned Hanlon
Games: 1267
At bats: 5074
Hits: 1317
Home runs: 30
Runs: 930
RBIs: 438
Batting Avg.: .260

Ned Hanlon and Frank Chance endorsed, Pennant Puzzle. L.W. Harding, 1909. 4" x 3.5". *From the Cooper collection.*

"E-E-Yah" Base Ball Game, c. 1910. Hughie Jennings is in a famous pose on the top of the this box. The title "E-E-Yah" was his trademark cheer as he coached third base for the Detroit Tigers. A spinner determines the play. The game came with a mailing box. National Games Company. 4.5" x 4.5". *From the Cooper collection.*

Tim Jordan
Games: 540
At bats: 1813
Hits: 474
Home runs: 32
Runs: 220
RBIs: 232
Batting Avg.: .261

Hughie Jennings
Games: 1285
At bats: 4903
Hits: 1532
Home runs: 18
Runs: 993
RBIs: 840
Batting Avg.: .312
Hall of Fame: 1945

T.J. Jordan Indoor Card Game, c. late 1910s. The game is made up of 72 cards with wonderful graphics, a small playing field, and wooden discs as men. Beside the game is an autographed photo of Tim Jordan, Brooklyn, National League, that did not come with the game. The "Tim" J. Jordan Playing Card Company. 6" x 3". *Courtesy of Bill Dlouhy.*

Frank "Home Run" Baker
Games: 1575
At bats: 5985
Hits: 1838
Home runs: 96
Runs: 887
RBIs: 1013
Batting Avg.: .307
Hall of Fame: 1955

Bob Bescher
Games: 1228
At bats: 4536
Hits: 1171
Home runs: 28
Runs: 749
RBIs: 345
Batting Avg.: .258

Roger Bresnahan
Games: 1430
At bats: 4480
Hits: 1253
Home runs: 26
Runs: 683
RBIs: 530
Batting Avg.: .280
Hall of Fame: 1945

Hal Chase
Games: 1917
At bats: 7417
Hits: 2158
Home runs: 57
Runs: 980
RBIs: 941
Batting Avg.: .291

Ty Cobb
lt>Games: 3034
At bats: 11429
Hits: 4191
Home runs: 118
Runs: 2245
RBIs: 1961
Batting Avg.: .367
Hall of Fame: 1936

Red Dooin
Games: 1290
At bats: 4004
Hits: 961
Home runs: 10
Runs: 333
RBIs: 344
Batting Avg.: .240

John Kling
Games: 1260
At bats: 4241
Hits: 1152
Home runs: 20
Runs: 475
RBIs: 513
Batting Avg.: .272

Nap Lajoie
Games: 2479
At bats: 9592
Hits: 3244
Home runs: 83
Runs: 1503
RBIs: 1599
Batting Avg.: .338
Hall of Fame: 1937

Tris Speaker
Games: 2789
At bats: 10208
Hits: 3515
Home runs: 117
Runs: 1881
RBIs: 1559
Batting Avg.: .344
Hall of Fame: 1937

Honus Wagner
Games: 2789
At bats: 10441
Hits: 3418
Home runs: 101
Runs: 1735
RBIs: 1732
Batting Avg.: .327
Hall of Fame: 1936

Bobby Wallace
Games: 2383
At bats: 8642
Hits: 2303
Home runs: 35
Runs: 1059
RBIs: 1121
Batting Avg.: .266
Hall of Fame: 1953

Walter Johnson
Games: 801
Wins: 416
Losses: 279
Pct.: .599
ERA: 2.17
Hall of Fame: 1936

Christy Mathewson
Games: 634
Wins: 373
Losses: 188
Pct.: .665
ERA: 2.13
Hall of Fame: 1936

Nap Rucker
Games: 336
Wins: 134
Losses: 134
Pct.: .500
ERA: 2.42

Ed Walsh
Games: 430
Wins: 195
Losses: 126
Pct.: .607
ERA: 1.82
Hall of Fame: 1946

Major League Indoor Base Ball, 1913. This game is probably the most desirable twentieth century player endorsed base ball game. It is actually a deluxe version of the more common "green lid" version. Players on the box top are: (top, left to right) Home Run Baker, Ty Cobb, Napoleon LaJoie, Ed Walsh, Tris Speaker, Hal Chase, Walter Johnson, and Bobby Wallace; (bottom, left to right) Christy Mathewson, Frank Chance, Honus Wagner, Charles "Red" Dooin, Roger Bresnahan, Bob Bescher, Nap Rucker, and John Kling. A complete game is comprised of two red boxes with player line-ups and pegs with painted faces. The envelopes are to hold pitcher and catcher cards after they were cut from the strips.Every season the Philadelphia Game Manufacturing Co. would publish new line-ups that could be purchased separately. Philadelphia Game Manufacturing Co. 20" x 13". *From the Cooper collection.*

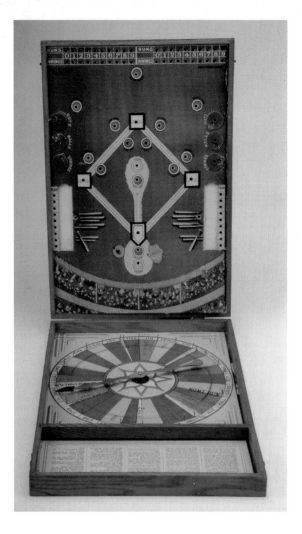

Inside of board.

Major League Indoor Base Ball, 1913. This is the generic version of the player endorsed game, but no players have lent their names to it. Philadelphia Game Manufacturing Co. 20" x 13". *From the Cooper collection.*

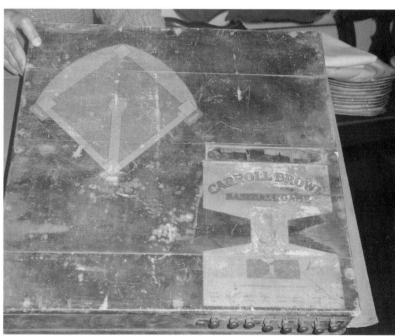

National Base Ball Puzzle-The Matty-Evers Game, 1913. The object of the puzzle is to have one ball (Mathewson) stay in the pitching mound, while the other ball (Evers) rounds the bases. Popular Games Company. 3" in diameter. *From the Cooper collection.*

Johnny Evers
Games: 1783
At bats: 6134
Hits: 1658
Home runs: 12
Runs: 919
RBIs: 538
Batting Avg.: .270
Hall of Fame: 1946

Carroll Brown Baseball Game, 1915. Knobs at bottom are pulled to activate a spinner mechanism. The results are revealed in the small windows. A Victrola mechanism is used to power the spinners. Wood, 20" x 20". *From the Cooper collection.*

Carroll "Boardwalk" Brown
Games: 133
Wins: 38
Losses: 40
Pct.: .487
ERA: 3.47

Pat Moran
Games: 819
At bats: 2634
Hits: 618
Home runs: 18
Runs: 198
RBIs: 262
Batting Avg.: .235

Pat Moran's Own Ball Game, 1919. There are two versions of this game. This one is a boxed game with a game board having nine spinners and a blank back. The choice of spinner depends on the play situation. Moran managed the Reds, who beat the Chicago Black Sox in the 1919 series. Smith, Kline, & French. 10" x 19". *From the Cooper collection.*

Walter Johnson Base Ball Game, c. 1920. A top has ten coins inside with the image of Walter Johnson. The top itself has many sides. The side that is up when it comes to rest determines the play. Great photo of Johnson in his Senator uniform is on the box top. Walter Johnson Baseball Game. 10" x 14.5". *From the Cooper collection.*

Pat Moran's Own Ball Game, 1919. The other version has a 4" x 4" implement box with pieces and instructions. The board has the same nine spinners, but the picture of Moran is on the back of the playing board. Smith, Kline, & French. 10" x 19". *From the Cooper collection.*

Walter Johnson Base Ball Game, late 1930s. A later version of the earlier game, the box cover has a photograph of Walter Johnson holding the earlier version in his hands. *From the Cooper Collection.*

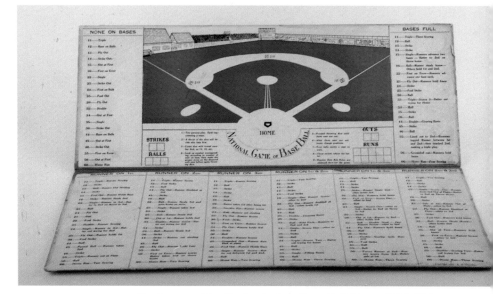

Babe Ruth
Games: 2503
At bats: 8399
Hits: 2873
Home runs: 714
Runs: 2174
RBIs: 2211
Batting Avg.: .342
Hall of Fame: 1936

Babe Ruth National Game of Baseball, 1921. A rare game using two die. On the back is a "sermon" by Rev. Bernard Clausen entitled "What Babe Ruth Teaches America." After comparing Ruth to ancient Greek sculpture and telling of his orphanhood and generosity, Clausen concludes, "In a world where a man is supposed to wear the proper pin on his vest, or speak the proper pass-word, or have the proper grip, or boast of graduation from the proper college, or wear the proper family name, or possess the proper blue-blood in the veins, before he can be admitted to the ranks of the favored ones, how much we need the lesson of a man who is not ashamed of a terribly poor start, and whose boast is that he made good with his own bare hands." Keiter-Fry Mfg. Co, Lockport, New York. 20" x 7.5" closed. *From the Cooper collection.*

Big League: The Perfect Indoor Base Ball Game, 1922. This game is endorsed by Connie Mack, Honus Wagner, and Ty Cobb. It uses two spinner boards to call the play. On the box top Connie Mack is quoted as saying, "I have played the game and enjoyed it thoroughly because it is complete in every detail...Every American home should have a copy of this game." G.L. Sibel. 10" x 15". *From the Cooper collection.*

Connie Mack
Games: 723
At bats: 2695
Hits: 659
Home runs: 5
Runs: 391
RBIs: 265
Batting Avg.: .245
Hall of Fame: 1937

John McGraw
Games: 1099
At bats: 3924
Hits: 1308
Home runs: 13
Runs: 1024
RBIs: 462
Batting Avg.: .333
Hall of Fame: 1937

Home Base Ball: The National Game, 1922. Played with 37 cards that have a likeness of Babe Ruth on the back. The plays on the cards are used to refer back to the inside of box top to determine the results. A card in the game offers to send a free game to the first person to report and error in the game. Endorsed on the box top by John McGraw, Buck Herzog, Jack Onslow, Eddie Dyer and others, the gamed also has a book of testimonials. Home Base Ball Corporation. 11" x 9". *From the Cooper collection.*

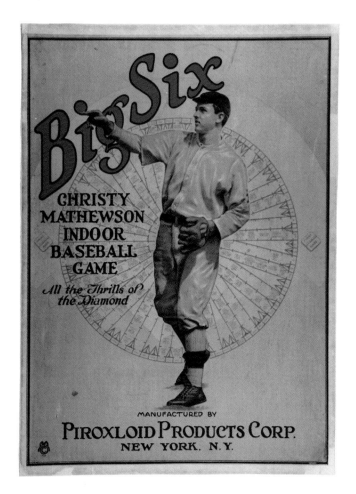

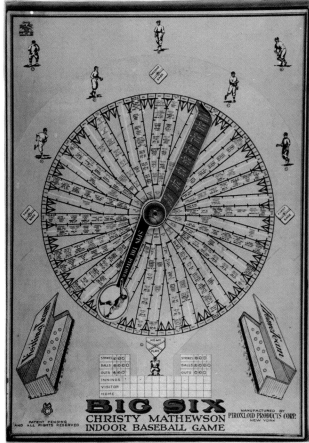

Big Six, Christy Mathewson Indoor Baseball Game, 1922. The box top has a beautiful picture of Mathewson. The board has a spinner with his image as the tip of the arrow. The game also included the line-up for the 1905 World Series, and the line-up of every team from the American and the National Leagues. An empty box bottom will hold the spinner board. Piroxloid Products Corp., New York. 23" x 17". *From the Cooper collection.*

Line up card for Big Six. *From the Cooper collection.*

Danny MacFayden's Stove League Baseball Game, 1927. Many versions of this game were made. This one is a bound book. The opponents sit on opposite sides of the open book. There are two dice, on going up to number 6 (red) and one to number 4 (green). The combination determine the play in a particular situation. Each situation has a number of options spelled out in the book. This boxed, hard back edition has a booklet of fans expressing their pleasure with this game, an instruction booklet, and player pieces. 11" x 16". *From the Cooper collection.*

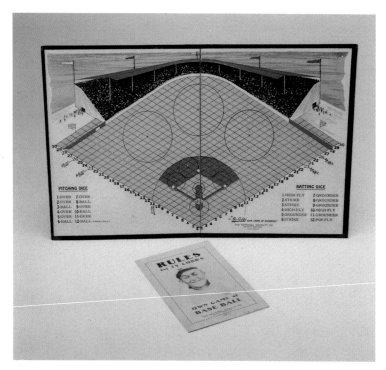

Ty Cobb's Own Game of Baseball, National Novelty Co., Detroit, 1924. An extremely rare dice game. The throw of the dice lands you on the grid which determines the play.l 13" x 10". *From the Cooper collection.*

Danny MacFayden
Games: 465
Wins: 132
Losses: 159
Pct.: .454
ERA: 3.96

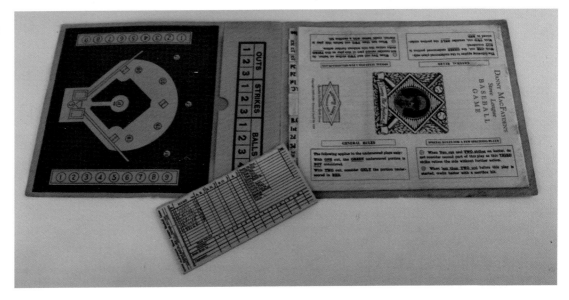

Waner's Baseball Game, 1930s. A card game with 61 cards, 23 offensive and 38 defensive. The board has two fields played simultaneously, one defense and one offense. Small metallic men and a score card accompany the game. Distributed by Waner's Baseball Inc. 9.5" x 15". *From the Cooper collection.*

Danny MacFayden's Stove League Baseball Game, 1929. This paper back edition plays the same as the earlier boxed edition, but has no players. It may have been designed for economy or for travel. National Games, Newtonville, Massachusetts. 8" x 11". *From the Cooper collection.*

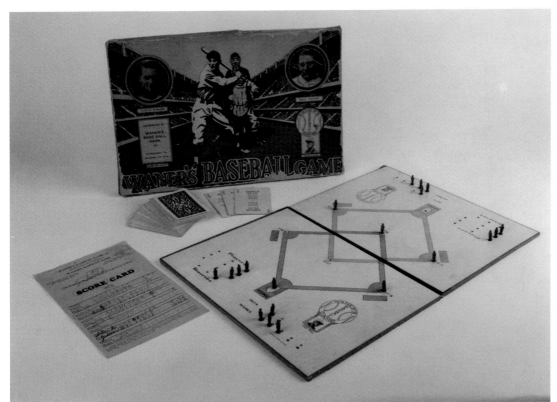

Lloyd Waner
Games: 1992
At bats: 7772
Hits: 2359
Home runs: 28
Runs: 1201
RBIs: 598
Batting Avg.: .316
Hall of Fame: 1967

Paul Waner
Games: 2549
At bats: 9459
Hits: 3152
Home runs: 112
Runs: 1626
RBIs: 1309
Batting Avg.: .333
Hall of Fame: 1952

The Lew Fonseca Baseball Game, 1930s. Wood, fiber board and net. Carrom Company, Ludington, Michigan. 27" x 27". On the back is a short history of Lew up to his position as director of promotions for the American League in the 1930s. *From the Cooper Collection, with cover courtesy of Marty and Debby Krim.*

Lew Fonseca	Home runs: 31
Games: 947	Runs: 518
At bats: 3404	RBIs: 485
Hits: 1075	Batting Avg.: .316

Bing Miller Base Ball Game, 1932. An exceedingly rare game, the marble is put against one of three openings in the guard wall and struck with a finger to put it in play. Where it lands determines the play. The box top has a facsimile autograph, and in this case there is an actual autograph beneath the facsimile. John P. Ryan Company. 12" x 16". *From the Cooper collection.*

Bing Miller
Games: 1821
At bats: 6212
Hits: 1937
Home runs: 117
Runs: 947
RBIs: 990
Batting Avg.: .312

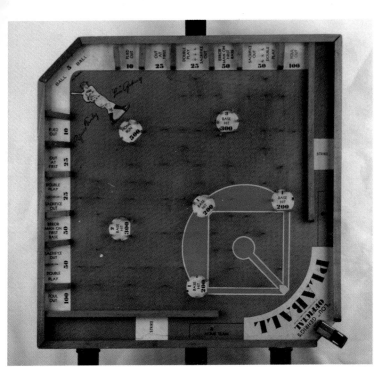

Lou Gehrig
Games: 2164
At bats: 8001
Hits: 2721
Home runs: 493
Runs: 1888
RBIs: 1990
Batting Avg.: .340
Hall of Fame: 1939

Tommy Bridges
Games: 424
Wins: 194
Losses: 138
Pct.: .584
ERA: 3.57

"Lou" Gehrig Official Play Ball, 1932. Bagatelle game in a pentagon shape with a shooter as the hitter at home plate. There is a four inch image of Gehrig batting with a facsimile autograph. The box to the game has never been found. Christy Walsh, 18" x 18". *From the Cooper collection.*

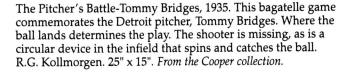

The Pitcher's Battle-Tommy Bridges, 1935. This bagatelle game commemorates the Detroit pitcher, Tommy Bridges. Where the ball lands determines the play. The shooter is missing, as is a circular device in the infield that spins and catches the ball. R.G. Kollmorgen. 25" x 15". *From the Cooper collection.*

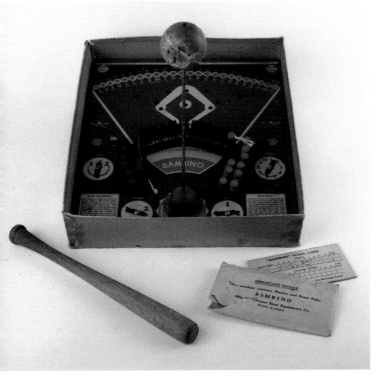

Bambino, mid-1930s. A metal on wood game. The ball on a rod is hit very hard and as it is knocked down the rod catches in a slot. Where it points determines the play. A rare version of this game has a cardboard fence that features a picture of Babe Ruth and advertises Babe Ruth's Bambino Ball Game. This rarer game measures 21" x 20". Johnson Store Equipment Co., Illinois. 14" x 12". *From the Cooper collection.*

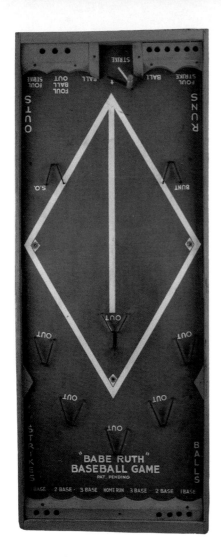

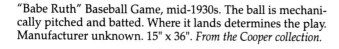

Goose Goslin
Games: 2287
At bats: 8655
Hits: 2735
Home runs:
Runs: 1483
RBIs: 1609
Batting Avg.
Hall of Fame

Goose Goslin's Scientific Baseball Game, 1935. A great photo of Leon Allen (Goose) Goslin with the clutch hit that won the 1935 World Series. It is a spinner game with discs that are used as players. Goslin's hit singled in Mickey Cochran in the bottom of the 9th to beat the Cubs 4-2. Wheeler Toy Company. 15" x 11". *From the Cooper collection.*

"Babe Ruth" Baseball Game, mid-1930s. The ball is mechanically pitched and batted. Where it lands determines the play. Manufacturer unknown. 15" x 36". *From the Cooper collection.*

Official Dizzy and Daffy Dean Nok-Out Baseball Game, c. mid-1930s. It came in a cardboard tube with a label that shows Dizzy and Daffy pithing. Rolled up inside was a 36" x 48" oil cloth playing field with seven paper men and a paddle used as a bat. Nok-Out Manufacturing Co., Wisconsin. Tube 38" long. *From the Cooper collection.*

Dizzy Dean
Games: 317
Wins: 150
Losses: 83
Pct.: .644
ERA: 3.02
Hall of Fame: 1953

Paul "Daffy" Dean
Games: 159
Wins: 50
Losses: 34
Pct.: .595
ERA: 3.75

Rube Bressler's Baseball Game, 1936. A four dice game where the total determines the outcome of the play. To sacrifice you use three dice. A combination score board and guide to the dice rolls. Ray B. Bressler, Inc. 6" x 10.5". *From the Cooper collection.*

Rube Bressler's Baseball Game, 1936. This version has a game board in addition to the accoutrements of the smaller version. On the inner box it says that "75% of money derived from advertising that might appear on the fences of this game will be donated to the baseball players' fraternity for old, needy baseball players." Ray B. Bressler, Inc. 25" x 12". *From the Cooper collection.*

Rube Bressler
Games: 1305
At bats: 3881
Hits: 1170

Home runs: 32
Runs: 544
RBIs: 586
Batting Avg.: .301

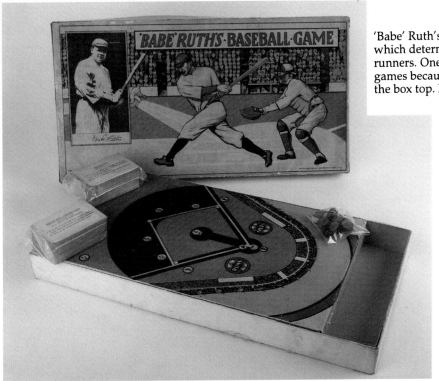

'Babe' Ruth's Baseball Game, 1936. Comprised of 85 cards which determine the situation and wooden pegs used as runners. One of the most popular of the Babe Ruth baseball games because of the facsimile autograph and his picture on the box top. Milton Bradley. 10" x 19". *From the Cooper collection.*

Ba-Be Baseball, 1937. Colored ball come in a cloth bag. A ball is removed from the bag without looking, and the color names the play. Carrmill Game Company, New York. 6" x 3". *From the Cooper collection.*

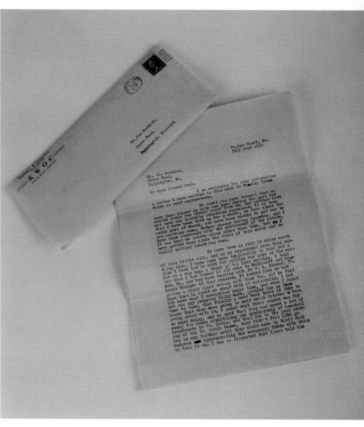

Letter from Herbert Johnston to Joe Medwick.

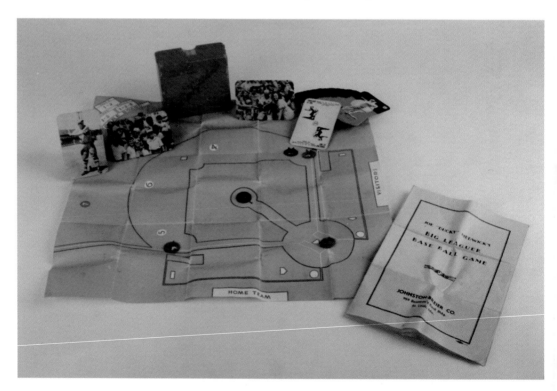

Joe Medwick
Games: 1984
At bats: 7635
Hits: 2471
Home runs: 205
Runs: 1198
RBIs: 1383
Batting Avg.: .324
Hall of Fame: 1968

Joe "Ducky" Medwick Big Leaguer Baseball Game, 1939. This card game was the commercially available edition of the prototype box game Johnston-Breier Co. produced in 1937 limited numbers. It has a vinyl fold-out field, sixty playing cards, along with three photographic cards of Medwick. Johnston-Breier Co. 3.5" x 4.5". *From the Cooper collection.*

Joe "Ducky" Medwick Big League Baseball Game, prototype. This may never have been manufactured for the marketplace, though a smaller version was introduced in 1939. This prototype belonged to Joe Medwick as the accompanying documentation indicates. A letter dated July 22, 1938, from Herbert B. Johnston, president of Johnston-Breier Company tells Medwick that the company they hired to market the game was not doing a great job, and suggesting that they and Medwick "cut out the middle man." It relays how the game had been played on the radio, with the effect of making listeners think that a real ball game was being broadcast. Johnston also says he sent copies of the game to Leo Durocher, Johnny Mize and a couple of other players may have had copies of the prototype. The playing field in the prototype is on cardboard. In the final version it is a vinyl material. The cards are identical. Johnston-Breier Co. 19" x 9". *From the Cooper collection.*

Carl Hubbell
Games: 535
Wins: 253
Losses: 154
Pct.: .622
ERA: 2.97
Hall of Fame: 1947

Bambino Baseball Game, 1946. A bat is used to hit the ball. Where it lands sets the play. There was a recent warehouse find of these games, which makes them relatively common. Mansfield-Zesiger Manufacturing, Ohio. 10" x 15". *From the Cooper collection.*

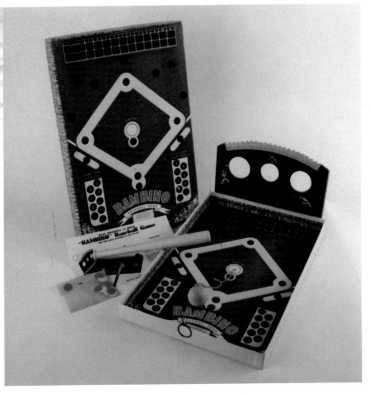

Strike 3 by Carl Hubbell, 1946. There are two versions of the Carl Hubbell Mechanical Baseball. This version is nearly identical to the later version, except that at the raised fielding positions it has letters instead of player graphics. Tone Products Corporation. 14.5" x 14.5". *From the Cooper collection.*

61

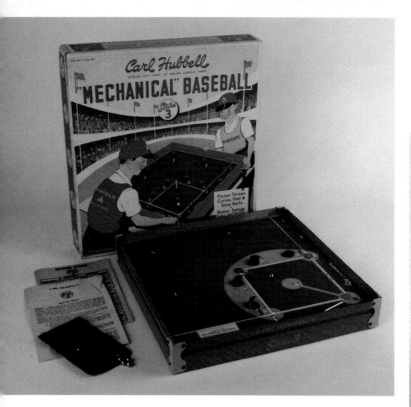

Hugh Casey
Games: 343
Wins: 75
Losses: 42
Pct.: .641
ERA: 3.45

Carl Hubbell Mechanical Baseball. The Gotham Pressed Steel Corporation version shown here has a colorful box and is the newer version. The balls are pitched by device that is controlled along the right field line, and the bat is spring action. The board is a metal structure with a felt field. It comes with official rules and score card. Gotham Pressed Steel Corp., New York. 14.5" x 14.5". *From the Cooper collection.*

Casey on the Mound, 1947. One of the most unusual games, it has a cardboard ball field with cut-out players. The ball is pitched by a person's hand through an opening in the center field wall, and the bat is held by the opponent's hand through an opening next to home plate. Hugh Casey is the player endorsing the game. Kamm Games Inc. 25" x 25". *From the Cooper collection.*

Close up of Casey on the Mound.

Additional parts to the Jackie Robinson game. *From the Cooper collection.*

Babe Ruth's Official Baseball Game, 1948. The box has images of Babe Ruth and Yankee Stadium on a red background. The game board has a wood frame with a felt covered cardboard surface. The complete game has a metal backstop, a Babe Ruth Official Game Flag pole, and a ceramic batter that is driven with a wire push cord. The metal ball is held by a magnet that hangs by a string from the pennant. The board has metal "catchers" at the infield positions, and cutouts around the outfield. The batter hits the ball, and where it lands determines the play. Toy Town Corporation, New York. 25" x 19". *From the Cooper collection.*

Jackie Robinson Baseball Game, 1948. A similar playing field to the earlier Carl Hubbell games without the felt playing field. Balls are pitched mechanically and hit by a spring loaded bat. Comes with a score card and rules for playing. It also comes with an 8" x 10" photograph of Robinson with a facsimile autographed. Gotham Pressed Steel Corporation. *From the Cooper collection.*

Jackie Robinson
Games: 1382
At bats: 4877
Hits: 1518
Home runs: 137
Runs: 947
RBIs: 734
Batting Avg.: .311
Hall of Fame: 1962

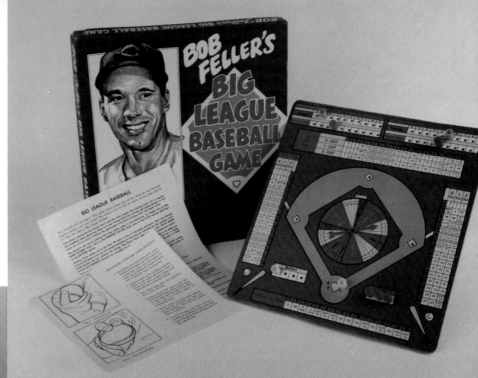

Bob Feller
Games: 570
Wins: 266
Losses: 162
Pct.: .621
ERA: 3.25
Hall of Fame: 1962

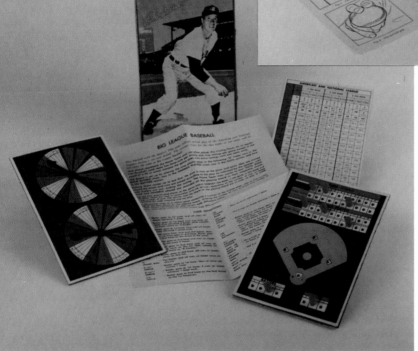

Bob Feller's Big League Baseball, 1949. This is the earlier of two versions of this game. This is a spinner game. In addition to the instruction sheet the game included "Bob Feller's Tips for Good Pitching. Saalfield Artcraft. 13" x 12". *From the Cooper collection.*

Bob Feller's Big League Baseball Game, 1950. This is the travel version of the game, an indication of te growing place the automobile had in post-war life. Saalfield Artcraft. 5" x 7.5". *From the Cooper collection.*

Bobby Shantz
Games: 537
Wins: 119
Losses: 99
Pct.: .546
ERA: 3.38

Bobby Shantz Magic Catcher, early 1950s. A velcro pitching target. Regent Games Incorporated. 10" x 31". *From the Cooper collection.*

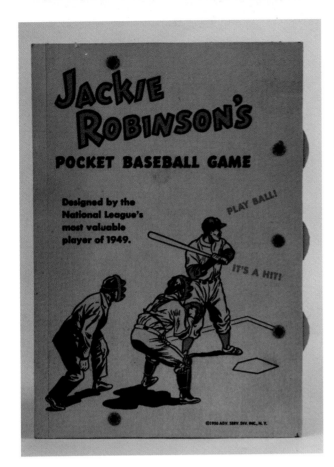

Jackie Robinson's Pocket Baseball Game, 1950. "Designed by the National League's Most Valuable Player for 1949." This cardboard book has a drawing of Jackie Robinson at bat and opens up to reveal a spinner game and score board. Advertising Services Division Inc., 6.5" x 4.5". *From the Cooper collection.*

Red Barber's Big League Baseball Game, 1950. This cult game is one of the most desired games of any of the player endorsed series. Apparently a limited edition from 500 to 1000 of these games were made, and possibly because of the popularity of radio announcer Red Barber and the pictured players, Burt E. Shotten, Tom Heinrick, Pee Wee Reese, Casey Stengel, Preacher Roe, and Carl Erskine, this is a favorite with New Yorkers. The game is comprised of a complex grid, and the roll of three dice determines the play. It comes with three dice, wooden pegs for the players. G & R Anthony, Inc., New York. 23" x 13". *From the Cooper collection.*

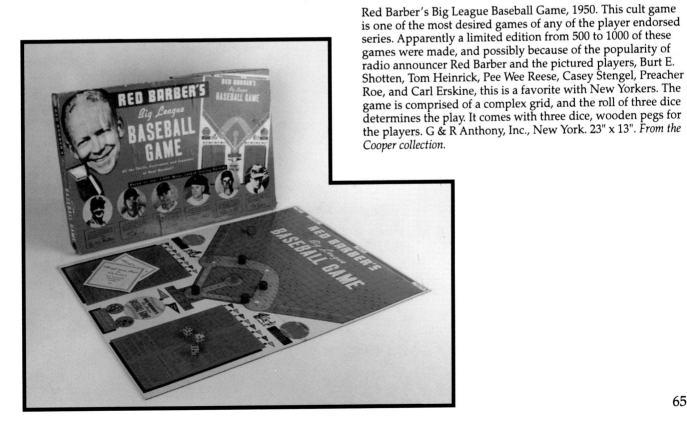

Hank Bauer
Games: 1544
At bats: 5145
Hits: 1424
Home runs: 164
Runs: 833
RBIs: 703
Batting Avg.: .277

Robin Roberts
Games: 676
Wins: 286
Losses: 245
Pct.: .539
ERA: 3.41
Hall of Fame: 1976

Be a Manager, 1953. Hank Bauer endorsed game designed by Sy Marder. The game uses three dice and player cards with lifetime averages of those mentioned, and play options for that player depending on the roll of the dice. Bamco Enterprises. 19" x 12.5". *From the Cooper collection.*

Say Hey! Willie Mays Baseball Game, 1954. Spinner game with fielding, pitching, and batting spinners. An important part of the game is the photograph with a facsimile signature of Willie Mays. There is also a scorecard. Toy Development Company. 14" x 9". *From the Cooper Collection.*

Robin Roberts Sports Club Baseball Game. 1952. A spinner determines the situation or directs you to draw a card to name the play. Interestingly the cards name Robert's Phillies team-mates as the playmakers. They also have a baseball fact. 19" x 13". *From the Cooper collection.*

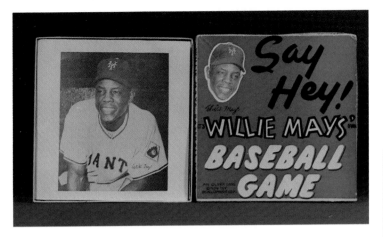

Willie Mays
Games: 2992
At bats: 10881
Hits: 3283
Home runs: 660
Runs: 2062
RBIs: 1903
Batting Avg.: .302
Hall of Fame: 1979

Say Hey! It's Willie Mays' Own Baseball Game, 1954. An Oliver Game Toy Development Co., product, it feature a 7" square box with a headshot of Mays in a New York Giants cap.The game has two Willie Mays Score Cards, 3 different 2.5" spinners which attach to light cardboard play sheets., 3 plastic markers. The folded board has a photo of Mays, and folds out to a green and white playing field. *Courtesy of Marty & DebbyKrim.*

Pee-Wee, 1950s. This boxed game features Pee-Wee Reese on the box top with a facsimile signature. The game has 12 marbles, a "Pee Wee Enterprises" pencil, a Pee-Wee score pad, instruction sheet and cardboard stand-up playing board. The object was to get the marbles into the slots calling for the highest amount of points. Pee Wee Enterprises. 10" x 20". *Courtesy of Marty & DebbyKrim.*

Pee Wee Reese
Games: 2166
At bats: 8058
Hits: 2170
Home runs: 126
Runs: 1338
RBIs: 885
Batting Avg.: .269
Hall of Fame: 1984

Bobby Shantz's Baseball Game, 1954. A card game with offensive and defensive cards. The batter "hits" by matching the pitch card drawn by the pitcher. Plastic players for each position and 42 cards are included, along with an 8 x 10 glossy with facsimile autograph of Bobby Shantz. Realistic Games Manufacturing Company. 18" x 13". *From the Cooper collection.*

Whirly Bird Play Catch Game, 1958. Warren Spahn endorsed this game. Shown are a boxed version and a rack version in plastic wrap. Both games are played the same way; a suction cup arrow is caught by a hand-held target. The plastic wrapped game shown here has an actual autograph of Spahn. Innovation Industries. Plstic version, 8" x 16", boxed version 10" x 10". *From the Cooper collection.*

Dizzy Dean's Batter-Rou Baseball Game, 1955. Double roulette batter-pitcher mechanism, where the final location of the ball on the roulette determines the play. Picture of Dizzy Dean and a facsimile autograph are in the center field of the playing board. Memphis Plastic Enterprises. 18" x 9.5" *From the Cooper collection.*

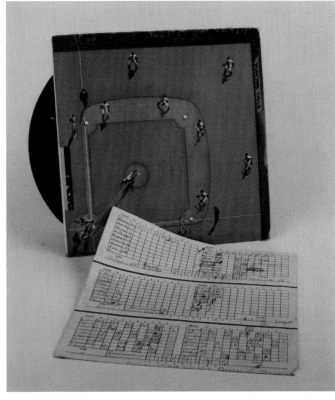

Mel Allen's Baseball Game, 1959. 33 1/3 rpm phonograph record with the plays announced by Mel Allen, with a playing field provided, so you can move players as the game progresses. RCA. 12" x 12". *From the Cooper collection.*

LA Dodgers Baseball Game, 1960. A card game with 70 cards, 51 green fielding cards and 19 red batting cards. The box top has individual photos of the Dodgers team members around the edge. These include Koufax, Drysdale, Hodges, and others. J & J Inc., California. 16.5" x 12". *From the Cooper collection.*

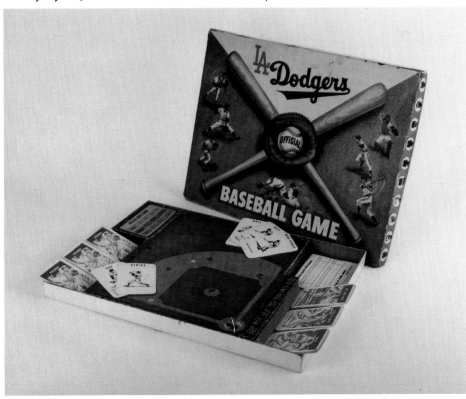

Sandy Koufax
Games: 397
Wins: 165
Losses: 87
Pct.: .655
ERA: 2.76
Hall of Fame: 1972

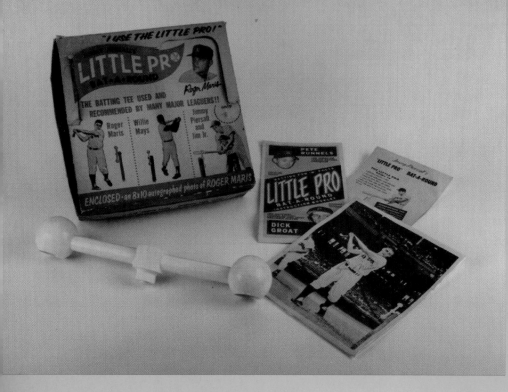

Jimmy Piersall's Little Pro Bat-a-Round, 1961. A hitting instructional device with endorsements by Dick Groat, Pete Runnels, Willie Mays, Jimmy Piersall, and an autographed photo of Roger Maris. Jimmy Piersall Inc., Massachusetts. *From the Cooper collection.*

Carl Yastrzemski Action Baseball, 1962. Pressman Toy Company. 15" x 20". *From the Cooper collection.*

Roger Maris Action Baseball, 1962. The tin and wood marble game came with a Pressman Times "newspaper" blurb about Maris being a home run king. Pressman Toy Company. 15" x 20". *From the Cooper collection.*

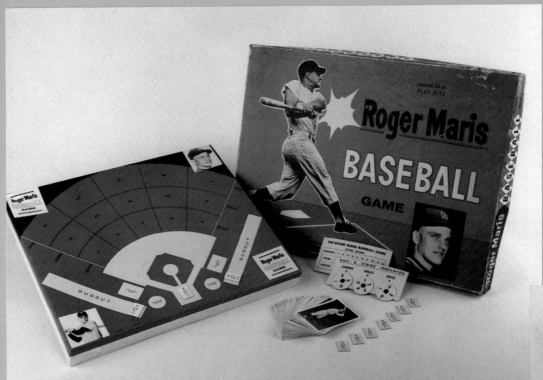

Roger Maris
Games: 1463
At bats: 5101
Hits: 1325
Home runs: 275
Runs: 826
RBIs: 851
Batting Avg.: .260

Mickey Mantle
Games: 2401
At bats: 8102
Hits: 2415
Home runs: 536
Runs: 1677
RBIs: 1509
Batting Avg.: .298
Hall of Fame: 1974

Roger Maris Baseball Game, 1962. A card game with die-cut fielders placed on various parts of the field. Defensively the object is arrange the players on the field so that if a batter draws a card that puts him in the same spot he will be out. Play-Rite. 19" x 11". *From the Cooper collection.*

Mickey Mantle's Big League Baseball, 1962. Dice game with roll determining play. The complete game includes dice cup with colored die, Mantle photograph with facsimile autograph, and play cards. Gardner & Company. 15" x 8". *From the Cooper collection.*

Big 6 Sports Games, 1959. Six games in one box, including Mickey Mantle's Big League Baseball, also sold separately. The other games are football, basketball, wrestling, stock car racing, and golf. Gardner & Co., Chicago. 20" x 15.5". *From the Cooper collection.*

71

Rocky Colavito
Games: 1841
At bats: 6503
Hits: 1730
Home runs: 374
Runs: 971
RBIs: 1159
Batting Avg.: .266

Mickey Mantle Baseball Action Game, 1960s. In this plastic game the ball is placed on the tee and Mickey hits it, by the player pressing a button. Where the ball lands determines play. There is a seven on the back of the figure, and Mickey's photo and directions underneath. A fairly rare piece. Kohner Brothers. 6" x 3". *From the Cooper collection.*

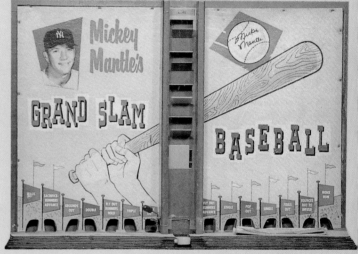

Mickey Mantle's Grand Slam Baseball Game, 1950s. Wood framed 6" x 21" x 15" game with instruction sheet on back. The marble is placed on the fipper and sent to the top of the tower. It returns at differing levels determining play. Gardiner and Co., Chicago. *Courtesy of Marty and Debby Krim.*

Mickey Mantle-Roger Maris Returno Pitch-N-Hit, early 1960s. A batting practice ball on a string, with facsimile autographs of Maris and Mantle. Returno Inc., New York. *From the Cooper collection.*

Rocky Colavito's Own Baseball Dart Game, 1960. This came with its own stand, or it could be mounted on the wall. On the reverse is a dart bowling game. Transogram Co., New York, New York. 256" x 22.5". *From the Cooper collection.*

Yogi Berra
Games: 2120
At bats: 7555
Hits: 2150
Home runs: 358
Runs: 1175
RBIs: 1430
Batting Avg.: .285
Hall of Fame: 1972

Yogi Berra Pitch Kit, 1963. Includes a 36" lifelike inflatable figure that supposedly resembles Yogi Berra, with four plastic balls to pitch into the inflatable glove over the cardboard home plate. "Kids and dad can't resist pitching." Ross Products. 11" x 8". *From the Cooper collection.*

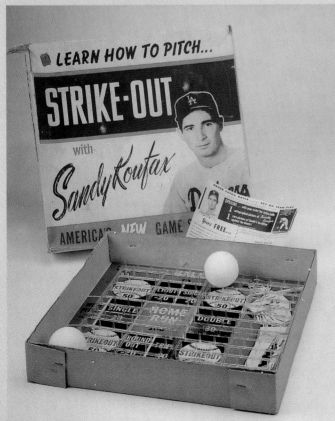

Strike Out with Sandy Koufax, Instructo Sports. Styrofoam balls are thrown at the target, which has plastic spikes to catch them. 16" x 16". 1963. This is extremely rare for a newer game. *From the Cooper collection.*

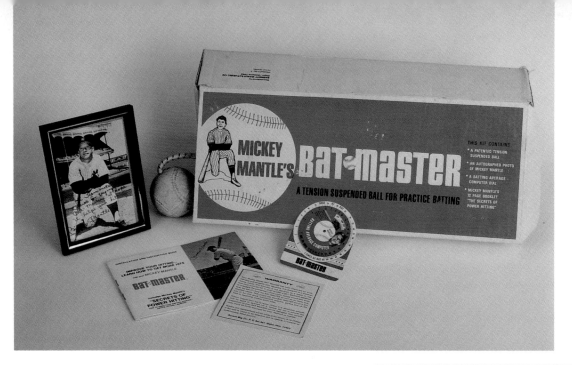

Mickey Mantle's Bat Master, 1964. A batting practice ball on a tension rope that can be hung from a pole or a tree, it came with a facsimile autographed photo, a batting instruction book, and a batting average "computer." There has been a recent find of these in a warehouse. Barnett Manufacturing, Oklahoma. 18" x 9". *From the Cooper collection.*

The Eye Ball, 1968. Endorsed by Hank Aaron, this is a ball on a rope used for teaching hitting. The back of the packing has all of Aaron's lifetime statistics up to that time. Fairmount Industries, Georgia. 6" x 8". *From the Cooper collection.*

Denny McLain Magnetik Baseball Game, 1968. Pressed steel action game by Gotham. 18" x 18". *From the Cooper collection.*

Tom Seaver
Games: 656
Wins: 311
Losses: 205
Pct.: .603
ERA: 2.86

Gil Hodges
Games: 2071
At bats: 7030
Hits: 1921
Home runs: 370
Runs: 1105
RBIs: 1274
Batting Avg.: .273

Tom Seaver Game Action Baseball, 1969. Another tin and wood action ball game, it came with pitching tips from Tom Seaver. Pressman Toy Company. 15" x 20". *From the Cooper collection.*

Gil Hodges' Pennant Fever, 1970. This game uses dice and fielding, batting, and pitching strategy cards. The combination of the dice and the cards sets the play. There is a line-up of all the major league players from both leagues. Research Games, Inc. 18" x 14". *From the Cooper collection.*

Hank Aaron Baseball Game, 1973. The ball is hit with the bat. Where it lands determines the play. If it is hit out of the park, the opponent has to catch it for an out. Ideal. 17.5" x 17.5". *From the Cooper collection.*

Boog Powell
Games: 2042
At bats: 6681
Hits: 1776
Home runs: 339
Runs: 889
RBIs: 1187
Batting Avg.: .266

John "Boog" Powell Pitch 'n Field, mid-1970s. A spring-net backstop for practice pitching. the ball bounces back to the thrower. Elcam Industries, New Jersey. 36" x 9". *From the Cooper collection.*

Johnny Bench
Games: 2158
At bats: 7658
Hits: 2048
Home runs: 389
Runs: 1091
RBIs: 1376
Batting Avg.: .267
Hall of Fame: 1989

Hank Aaron's Bases Loaded, 1976. A baseball trivia game. The player moves around the board by dice throw and is asked questions from the a trivia question book supplied with the game. Twentieth Century Enterprises. The box top has a photo of Aaron in front of a photo of Babe Ruth. 20" x 10". *From the Cooper collection.*

Whitey Herzog's Great Game of Baseball, 1976. Came with score sheets, a score board and a list of all the major league players of 1976. There are batter and fielder spinners that call the play. Blue Valley Manufacturing Co. 16" x 12". *From the Cooper collection.*

Johnny Bench Batter Up, late 1970s. A ball on a revolving stand for batting practice. Fonas Corporation, Pennsylvania. 50" x 6". *From the Cooper collection.*

Whitey Herzog
Games: 1493
At bats: 5284
Hits: 1370
Home runs: 20
Runs: 705
RBIs: 445
Batting Avg.: .259

Ernie Banks
Games: 2528
At bats: 9421
Hits: 2583
Home runs: 512
Runs: 1305
RBIs: 1636
Batting Avg.: .274
Hall of Fame: 1977

Ernie Banks' Ball 'n Strike, 1977. An instructional 33 1/3 rpm record, and a ball on a twenty foot rope, designed to teach hitting. "Dad (or Mom) and the boys can have a ball." FCE Company, California. 10" x 8". *From the Cooper collection.*

George Brett
Games: 2137
At bats: 8148
Hits: 2528
Home runs: 267
Runs: 1300
RBIs: 1311
Batting Avg.: .310

Brett Ball: George Brett's Ninth Inning Baseball Game, 1981. Copyright, Raymond O. Kelter, M.D. A dice game with a complicated slide-rule type indicators of play. Comes with a board, score cards, player pieces, and instructions. Brett Ball. 19" x 10". *From the Cooper collection.*

George Brett Baseball Stride Trainer, 1983. The game has vinyl images of footprints that teach the batter how to stride. Scharper Manufacturer. 18" x 17". *From the Cooper collection.*

Chapter 7

20th Century Non-Endorsed Games

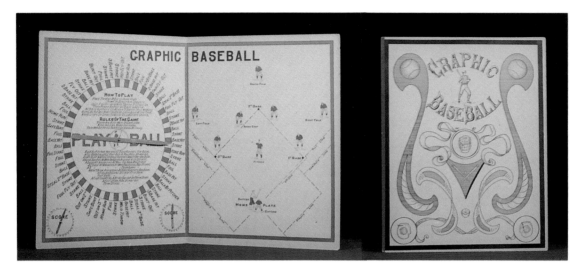

Graphic Baseball, early 20th century. The cover has eloquent graphics, featuring baseball equipment and a player of the period. The board opens to 14" x 22". On the left side is a large spinner inside a circle that has rules of the game in the center and possible play outcomes around the perimeter. On the right is a lithographed ball field with players but no umpire. C.E. Varney, Boston. 11" x 14". *Courtesy of Marty and Debby Krim.*

Base Ball Game Puzzle, c. early 20th century. The purpose of the game is to get the red jumping beans into the nine positions and to get the white umpire bean into his position last. Satis-Factory Company, Chicago. 3.5" x 6". *From the Cooper collection.*

Parlor Base Ball, 1903. The earlier of two versions of this game. With its red, white, and blue graphics this game has a very patriotic look to it. It is played with a single die, which has "O" on two sides for outs, and numbers 1-3 and HR on the other sides for hits. The box is dark blue cardboard. American Parlor Base Ball Company. 12" x 10". *From the Cooper collection.*

Parlor Base Ball, c. late 1910s. This later version has a red box with the same graphics on the box top and board. It is in a red box. Designed in the U.S.A., it was manufactured at the Spearworks in Bavaria. 15" x 11". *From the Cooper collection.*

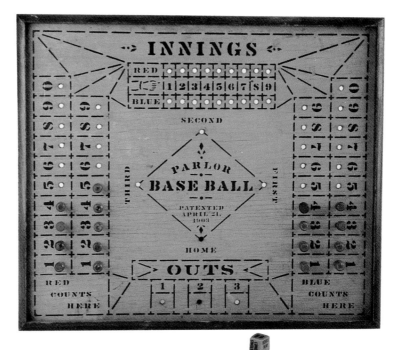

Parlor Base Ball, 1903. A wooden version of the dice game, with the same patent date, April 21, 1903. A checker board is on the opposite side. American Parlor Base Ball. 14" x 12". *From the Cooper collection.*

Peg Base Ball, 1908. This edition came in two versions, one with a yellow box and one with a blue. These are the earliest of three editions of the game, and use a single die to determine the play. Parker Brothers. 12" x 11". *From the Cooper collection.*

Peg Base Ball Game, 1936. This updated version follows the same single die roll structure, but the graphics are updated, representing a more complete playing field. Parker Brothers. 15" x 11" *From the Cooper collection.*

Game of Peg Baseball, 1961. The most recent version of peg baseball has a player who looks like Ted Williams. The graphics again are changed, and the play is more complicated, using the combinations of two dice. Parker Brothers. 15" x 11". *From the Cooper collection.*

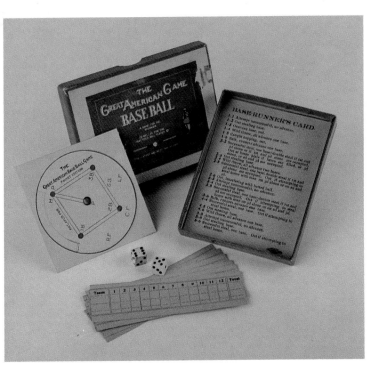

The Great American Base Ball Game, 1906. This dice game is also referred to as the Harvard-Yale game because the two figures on the front have H and Y on their sweaters. The field turns to color the bases with players on them. A Base Runners Card interprets the dice throws into plays. William Dapping. 4.5" x 3.5". *From the Cooper collection.*

Leslie's Base-Ball Game, 1909. A game with 85 playing cards. It also came with score book and a field of play. Both the score book and the field have advertising for Koch's Clothing. Perfection Novelty and Advertising Co., 14" x 11". *From the Cooper collection.*

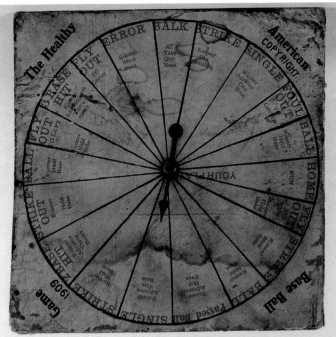

The Healthy American Base Ball Game, 1909. A spinner game that had no board. Manufacturer unknown. 7.5" x 7.5". *From the Cooper collection.*

An advertising game for the Coston Company, 1909. Marble game with holes in field. 9" x 9". *Courtesy of Mike Brown.*

81

Game of Base Ball, 1910. A spinner game where the number of the spin is the number of spaces moved around the diamond. On the left is the front of the box and on the right is the playing field. Milton Bradley. 7" x 7". *From the Cooper collection.*

Base Ball, 1910. The spinning top in this game determines play by the hole where it stops. The graphics are great, including the bench, where the player pieces are stored, and Hughie Jennings doing his cheer at third base. The Tigers are at bat. Pan-American Toy Co. 9" x 9". *From the Cooper Collection.*

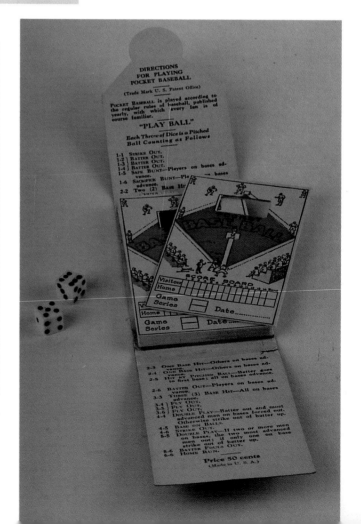

The Great American Game of Pocket Base Ball, 1910. A dice game to fit in the pocket. Neddy Pocket Game Company, New York. 2.5" x 4". *From the Cooper collection.*

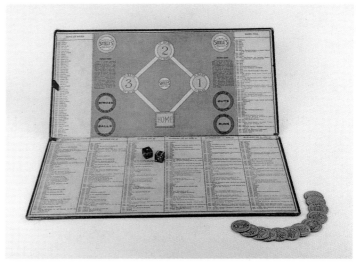

Steele's Inside Base Ball, 1911. A three dice board game with metal rimmed discs. ONly the board is shown. Steele Manufacturing. 18" x 9". *From the Cooper collection.*

Home Base Ball Game, 1911. An unusual hitting device puts the ball in play. The McLoughlin graphics of 1911, while still dramatic, do not measure up to the chromolithographic process of the 19th century, McLoughlin Brothers. 23" x 16". *From the Cooper collection.*

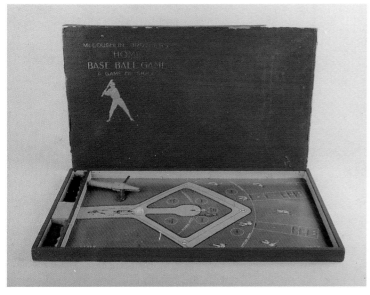

Home Base Ball Game, 1911. This is the same game as the previous 1911 McLoughlin game with slight color variations on the board, and a different box top. McLoughlin Brothers. 23" x 17". *From the Cooper collection.*

Auto-Play Baseball Game, 1911. The game came with a photo book with player endorsements. Each coin has the name of a player from the National or American League, with 14 or 15 players from each team. The game could be bought in either an American or National League version. Very similar to Inside Baseball, which depicted the 1913 World Series. Although they were made by different companies, replication must have taken place. Auto-Play Games Company, 19" x 17". *From the Cooper collection.*

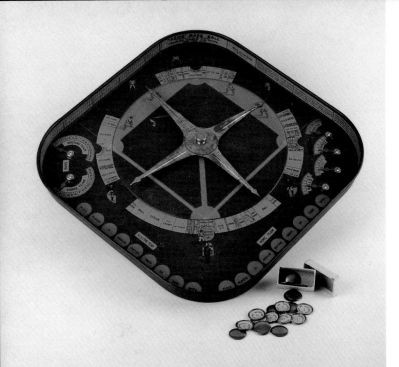

Inside Base Ball, 1913. A beautiful lithographed tin playing board and spinner, it has metal discs with the name, position and team of the players in the 1913 World Series between the Giants and the Athletics. The discs are exceeding rare, and the box they came in is even rarer. Popular Games Company, New York. 13" x 13". A larger, 18" x 18" version was also made. *From the Cooper collection.*

Promotional brochure for "Inside" Baseball with endorsements and facsimile autographs of John G. King, Boston-National; R. W. Fard, New York-American; Hugh Huffy, Chicago-American; Larry McLean, Cincinnati; Hal Chase, New York-American; P. J. Donovan, Boston-American; Hugh Jennings, Detroit-American; R.J. Wallace, St. Louis-American; Fred C. Clarke, Pittsburg-National; C. Mathewson, New York-National; Hans Wagner, Pittsburg-National; Fred Tenney, Boston-National; John J. McGraw, New York-National; Chas. S. Dooin, Philadelphia-National; Frank Chance, Chicago-National; and, most prominently, Ty Cobb. c. 1912. *Courtesy of Bruce Dorskind.*

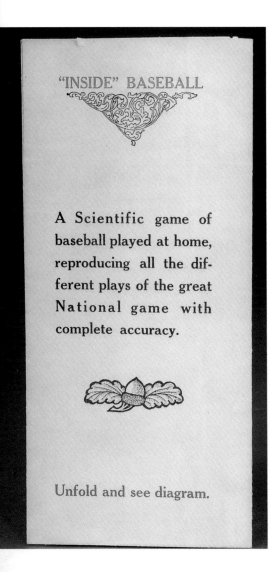

"INSIDE" BASEBALL

A Scientific game of baseball played at home, reproducing all the different plays of the great National game with complete accuracy.

Unfold and see diagram.

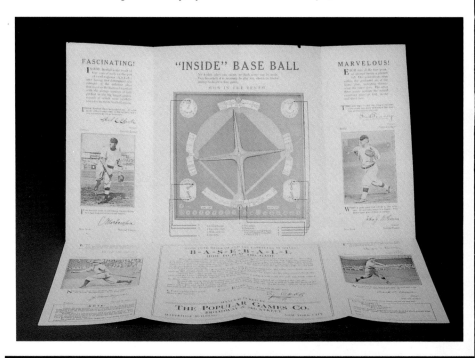

Grand-Stand Base Ball, c. 1912. This advertising game for Pluto Water, America's Greatest Physic "for constipation, liver, stomach, & kidney troubles". It features the devil in the center of the spinner and bases around. The spinner determines play. The game cost 25 cents. Pluto Water. 7" x 7". *From the Cooper collection.*

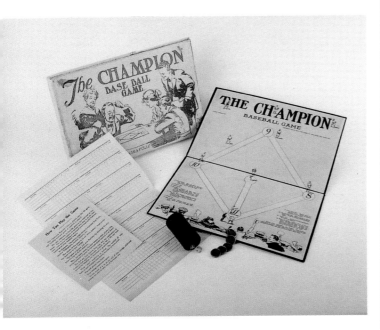

The Champion Baseball Game, 1913. A dice game. New York Game Company. 12" x 8". *From the Cooper collection.*

Home Diamond: The Great National Game, 1913. Two manufacturers produced this game at the same time, one on the east coast, one on the west. A metal ball runs down a field of metal barriers, with its final location determining the play. The pink version is by Phillips Company, New York and the green version is by Play Ball Game Company, San Francisco. 7.5" x 10.5". *From the Cooper collection.*

Fan-I-Tis, 1913. Copyright by C.W. Marsh. Dice game where combinations determine the play of the game. *From the Cooper collection.*

Grebnelle Base Ball Parlor Game, 1914. The regular version of the game. Grebnelle Novelty Co. 23" x 9" closed. *From the Cooper collection.*

Grebnelle Championship Base Ball Parlor Game, 1914. There are two versions of the Grebnelle Base Ball Parlor Game. This deluxe version has a photograph of the 1914 Boston Braves, National League and World's Champions, and the placard on the score board talks about the "Champions' Ball Park, Boston, 1914". The field on the box top is actually the Boston field. The game board is marked "American League Champions Ball Park 1914, Phila." Grebnelle was from Philadelphia. Both versions have a list of the names of 2000 players from 1914, in the National League, American League, Federal League, and various minor leagues. There are also rules, directions, explanations, score cards, average cards, a spinner, and player discs with metal rims for each position on each team. Grebnelle Novelty Co. 23" x 9" closed. *From the Cooper collection.*

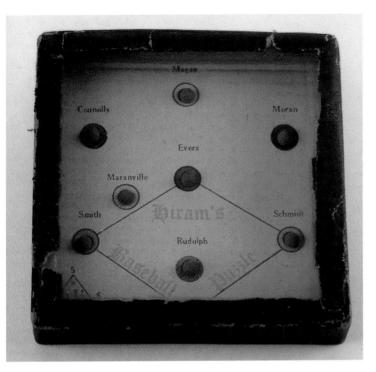

Hiram's Baseball Puzzle, c. 1914. The goal was to get the balls in the various playing positions. They are marked with the names of 1914 Boston Braves players, including Evers and Maranville. Hiram. 3.5" x 3.5". *From the Cooper collection.*

The Champion Game of Base Ball, 1915. Spinner game with discs as players. A relatively common game because of a recent find of these in a warehouse. Note that base ball is two words. It became one word sometime after World War I. Proctor Amusement, Massachusetts. 9" x 10". *From the Cooper collection.*

"Indoor Sports" Base Ball, 1915. A marble is dropped from home plate and goes through pins until it comes at rest to name the play. Palace Toy Co., Massachusetts. 5" x 8". *From the Cooper collection.*

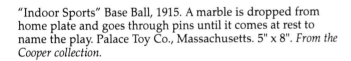

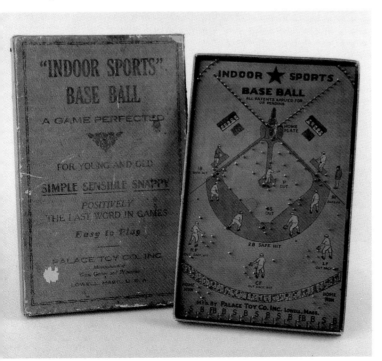

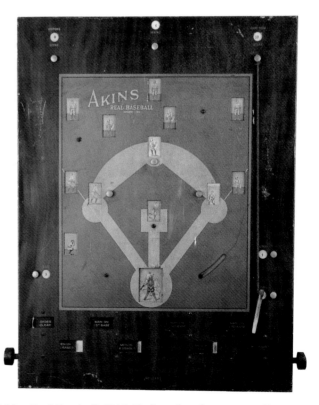

Akins Real Baseball, 1915. Tin board with paper scrolls. Turning the scroll changes the play options behind the doors at the bottom of the board. The player opens one door at a time to reveal the play. The score is kept in the boxes at the top, and the players can be changed to the correct team by moving knobs or letters. Akins Manufacturing Co. 19" x 24". *From the Cooper collection.*

Home Team Baseball Game, 1917. This is the first of four versions of this game. It has three spinners, one for fielding, one for batting and one for the umpire. Selchow & Righter. 19" x 13". *From the Cooper collection.*

Home Team Base Ball Game. The second version of this three spinner game, "Governed by the rules of Organized Base Ball." It is similar to the first, except that the box is less wide, there is a field on the game board, and the graphic on the box top has more photo-realism to it. The defensive spinner on the left has a player figure, the offensive has a wooden ball on a wire. In the center is the umpire who "decides all arguments." Copyrighted by Ben Dickenson, 1917. 9" x 19". *From the Cooper collection.*

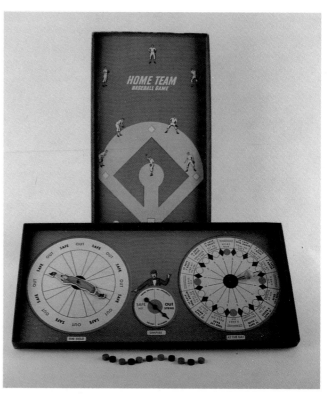

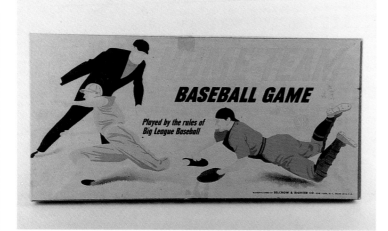

Home Team Baseball Game, 1938. The third version is more sophisticated, with the playing field on the inside of the box top. The action stays the same. The box top has the same theme of a player sliding into home with the catcher and ump present. Selchow & Righter. 20" x 10". *From the Cooper collection.*

Home Team Baseball Game, 1964. The game is simplified with into a single spinner game. Selchow & Righter. 16" x 9" *From the Cooper collection.*

World Series Baseball Game, 1916. An eight spinner game, with spinners for fielding, hitting and pitching. The game came with an offer of a monthly prize of $25 for the best letter about the game. Copyrighted by Clifford E. Hooper. United Games, Massachusetts 14" x 9". *From the Cooper collection.*

Play Ball, c. late 1910s. A nine spinner game used to determine the outcome of every possible baseball situation. The photo used is of undetermined origin. National Games Co., Inc., Boston. 14" x 17". *From the Cooper collection.*

Baseball and Checkers: Two Game Combination, c. late 1910s. Milton Bradley, having bought McLoughlin, used their graphics for this game, along with a McLoughlin spinner. Milton Bradley. 17" x 9". *From the Cooper collection.*

Big League Baseball at Home, 1920s. Spinner game the size of a silver dollar. Manufacturer unknown. 1.5" diameter. *From the Cooper collection.*

Armstead's Play Ball: A Game for Everyone, c. late 1910s. The dice from this game have symbols that set the play. J.I. Austin Co. 8.5" x 15". *From the Cooper collection.*

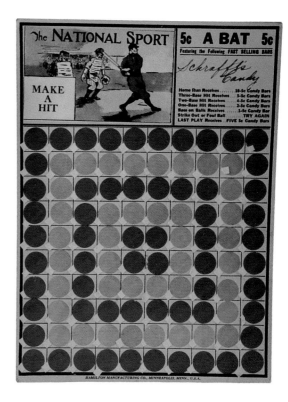

National Sport, 1920s. Advertising punch board. For 5 cents you could pick a dot. If you were lucky to get a home run you won ten 5 cent candy bars. If you were not so lucky you would get an out or foul ball and get nothing for your nickel. The piece could be used for any brand of candy the dealer chose. In this case someone has written Schrafft's Candy on the card. 7" x 10". *From the Cooper collection.*

Gambling game, c. late 1910s. A player's bet was placed in the slot of the favored team. Two dice are in the domed spinner. One die has the letters of the teams to be wagered upon, Yankees, Cubs, Giants, Athletics, Senators, and Braves. The other die is numbered, representing the turn on the bet. If the better's team came up on the die he would win and his bet would be multiplied by the number on the second die. Manufacturer unknown. 9" x 4". *From the Cooper collection.*

The Pocket Base Ball Game, 1921. The metal top with two independently moving parts sets the play. Occult Company. 1.25" tall. *From the Cooper collection.*

Slugger: A Real Baseball Game, 1920s. The throw of the dice guides you through the plays listed on the inside of the booklet. Manufacturer unknown. 9" x 12". *From the Cooper collection.*

Major League Ball, 1921. A dice game. This is an interesting game because each season a new set of die cut players could be purchased. The players wear team uniforms and came with labels that were attached to their bases, including player's name, position, batting order, left or right handed, etc. Note the team names on the envelopes: the Philadelphia Quakers and the Brooklyn Robins. National Game Makers, Washington, D.C. Open board size: 19" x 19". *From the Cooper collection.*

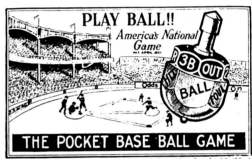

904—BASEBALL TOP—A regular game of baseball can be played with this top. Every play known in baseball can be made. Number of players is unlimited.

Advertisement for the Pocket Base Ball Game.

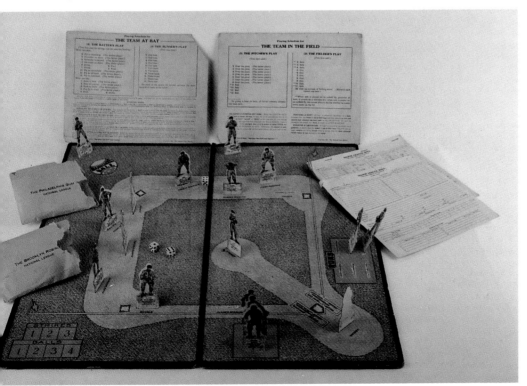

"Follow the Stars", 1922. The game book has the line-up of the entire national league with the actual players for 1922. It is a three dice game. The scoreboard comes with printed team names. H. Allen Watts. 9" x 12". *From the Cooper collection.*

The Great American Game, 1925. A tin and wood game with revolving scroll that calls the play. The earlier version was made by Frantz Toys, and the later version by Hustler Toy Corporation, which had purchased Frantz Toys. Both have a "Frantz Garage Hardware, Sterling, Ill." sign in left field. The box is probably twice as valuable as the gameboard. Frantz Toys and Hustler Toy Corporation. 9.5" x 14". *From the Cooper collection.*

All-American "Big Boy" Baseball game. Rosensteel-Pulich Co., 1922. 12" x 9". *From the Cooper collection.*

Double Game Board, c. 1926 & 1948. Though separated by a number of years, the main changes in these two games are in the box top and some updating to the baseball field. The earlier version is on the left. A basic dice baseball game. Parker Brothers. 17" x 9". *From the Cooper collection.*

Roll-O Junior Baseball Game, mid-1920s. Three wooden dice, two with numbers for offense and one with numbers for defense, name the play. There are elaborate metal figures in two colors of uniforms. Rollo Manufacturing, New York. 4.5" x 4.5". *From the Cooper collection.*

Book styled base ball games, 1928-1934. These book styled travel base ball games came in various colors. They are wood with a leatherette box top, and had a drawer containing the spinner and other game paraphernalia. Manufacturers include Drueke and Metro. Size 4.5" x 4.5". *From the Cooper collection.*

93

Dicex Base Ball Game, 1925. The score sheet has the line-ups of the 1925 World Series. 6" x 10". Chester S. Howland. *From the Cooper collection.*

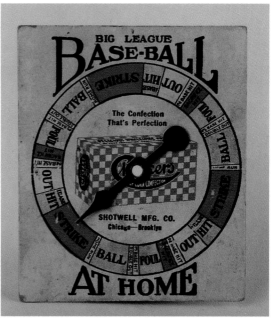

Big League Baseball, 1929. A spinner baseball game that is actually an advertisement for Checkers Popcorn Confection. Shotwell Manufacturing Company. 2.75" x 3.25". *From the Cooper collection.*

Diceball, 1928. The smallest baseball game known to exist, it has two dice with the various play situations. Dice Ball Co. 1.5" x 1.5". *From the Cooper collection.*

Roulette Base Ball Game, 1929. A spinner game shown in the boxed version and in a smaller tin version, probably later. William Bartholomae. Boxed version, 7" x 10"; metal version 3.5" x 5". *From the Cooper collection.*

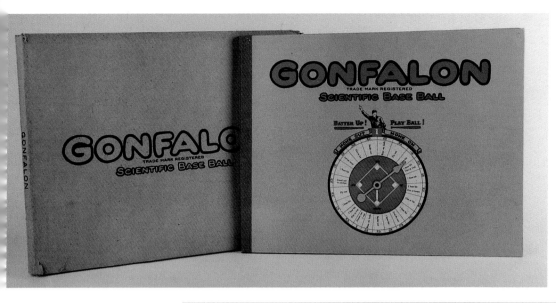

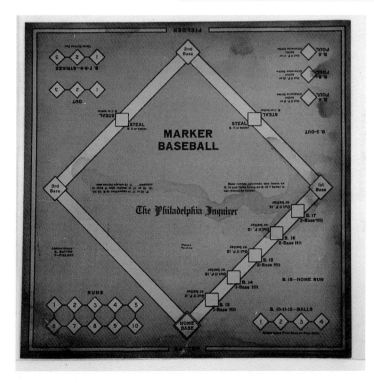

Gonfalon: Scientific Base Ball, c. early 1930s. This game has the most spinners of any known game with 24. There is a spinner for every situation. General Specialties Corporation. 14" x 18". *From the Cooper collection.*

Marker Baseball, The Philadelphia Inquirer, c. early 1930s. *From the Cooper collection.*

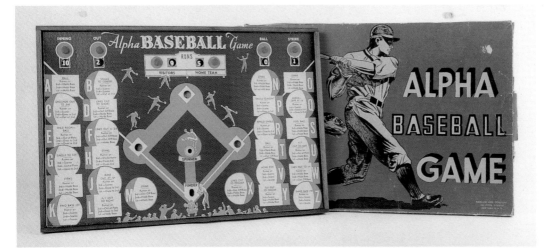

Alpha Baseball Game, c. 1930. A spinner in the pitchers mound directs you to instructions by the letter that comes up. Redlich Manufacturing. 20" x 13". *From the Cooper collection.*

The New Game of Home 'Baseball', 1939. The same game as the earlier Game of Baseball by this company, but with a new name and slightly revised graphics. Canada Games Company, Toronto.13" x 7". *From the Cooper collection.*

Game of Baseball, 1932. One of two Canadian baseball games. This is a dice game with a board. The rules are printed in French and English. Canada Games Company, Toronto. 11.5" x 6". *From the Cooper collection.*

Sportmaster: The Game of Games, 1933. The baseball game is one of six boards in this set. The spiral roulette wheel at the center sends the ball out into the a slot marked with the play. The roulette template changes for each game. Best Manufacturing. 18" x 18". *From the Cooper collection.*

Baseball Game, 1935. Snap the ball with a finger to determine the play. Cutler & Saleeby, Inc., Massachusetts. 13" x 8". *From the Cooper collection.*

Guyro Pocket Baseball, mid-1930s. The spinner and the dice work in combination to set the play. Harold Alexander Co. 4" x 4". *From the Cooper collection.*

Red Bird Baseball Game, mid-1930s. A small metal ball is hit by a spinning batter. The hole it falls into names the play. The game with the box is rare and most likely commemorates the St. Louis Cardinals. Measuregraph Co., St. Louis. 5" x 5". *From the Cooper collection.*

Big League Baseball Game, 1935. A game played with Tiddledy Winks. Whitman Publishing Co., Wisconsin. 12" x 9".

Official Radio Baseball Game, c. mid-1930s. Spinner game, with printed team names and numbers to hang on the score board and pegs to mark the base runners. Toy Creations, New York. 20" x 12" *From the Cooper collection.*

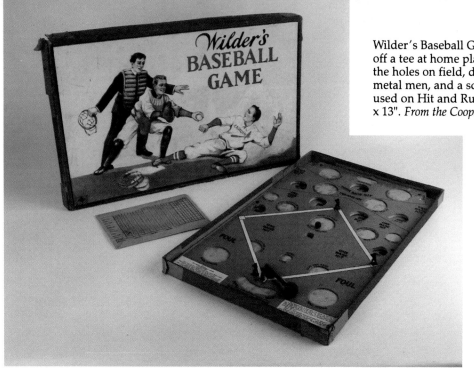

Wilder's Baseball Game, c. 1936. The round ball is propelled off a tee at home plate by a spring-action bat. It falls into one of the holes on field, determining the play. The game comes with metal men, and a score card. The same box top graphic was used on Hit and Run Baseball, 1938. Wilder Manufacturing. 22" x 13". *From the Cooper collection.*

Slide Kelly!, 1936. All I have of the game is the board. The roll of a red and yellow die makes the play. Slide Kelly Slide! was a famous phrase in reference to the great 19th century player Mike "King" Kelly. Be Ruth Co., New York. Board folded size: 20" x 10". *From the Cooper collection.*

Roll 'Em Ball Gum, 1936. Gum originally came in the boxes. When the gum was gone, the box became a rolling game piece to determine plays. Various situations required various colored boxes, so you needed a set. Goudy Gum Company. Each box 1" x 1" x 1". *From the Cooper collection.*

Home Baseball Game, 1936. Discs are thrown at the target from six feet away. If the disc lands on a line it counts as an out, as does any disc that lands outside of the target. Rosebud Art Company, New York. 9" x 9". *From the Cooper collection.*

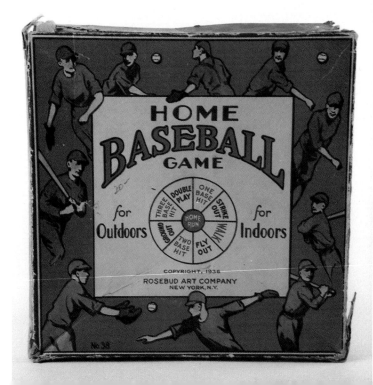

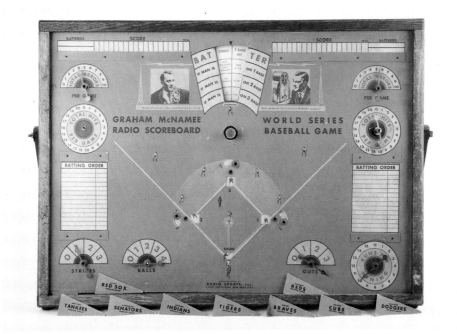

Graham McNamee Radio Scoreboard World Series Baseball Game, 1937. This game came in a generic cardboard box. Play is set by spinning the radio dial. On the other side is the Knute Rockne Football Game. The game came with pennants. Radio Sports Inc. 25" x 18". *From the Cooper collection.*

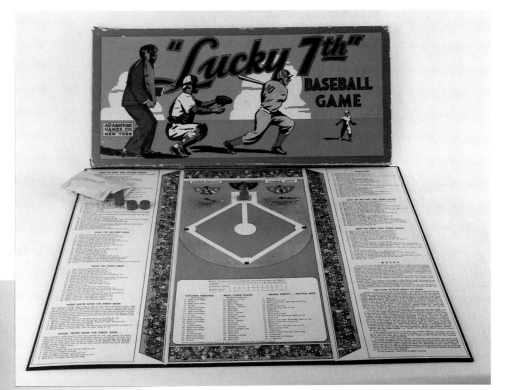

"Lucky 7th" Baseball Game, 1937. Dice game with board. All-American Games Company. 21" x 9". *From the Cooper collection.*

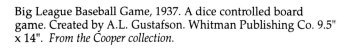

Big League Baseball Game, 1937. A dice controlled board game. Created by A.L. Gustafson. Whitman Publishing Co. 9.5" x 14". *From the Cooper collection.*

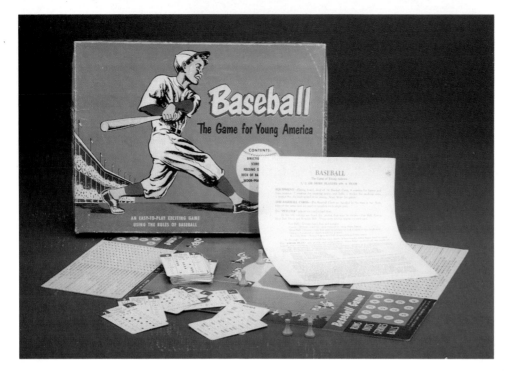

Baseball: The Game for Young America. Essentially a card game, the defensive players announces the type of pitch he is throwing. The offensive player pulls the top card off the deck and reads the result of the pitch on the Pitch side. If it results in a field play, the offensive player turns the card over and finds the result in the particular circumstance his team is in. E.E. Fairchild Corporation, Rochester, New York. 10.5" x 14.5". *From the Cooper collection.*

Hit and Run Baseball Game, c. 1938. The play is determined by flicking a disc ("ball") from home plate with a finger. The field is marked with various plays. The player sliding on the box top is purported to be Pepper Martin. The same box top graphic was used on Wilder Baseball, 1936. Wilder Manufacturing, 12" x 8". *From the Cooper collection.*

The Game of Friendly Fun, 1939. The animals get in the act on the box top of this game, but the insides really have nothing to do with baseball. Milton Bradley. 13.5" x 10.5". *From the Cooper collection.*

Baseball Bank Game, 1940s. A coin placed in the banks turns a wheel that gives the play. Manufacturer unknown. 3" in diameter. *From the Cooper collection.*

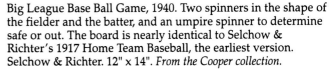

Big League Base Ball Game, 1940. Two spinners in the shape of the fielder and the batter, and an umpire spinner to determine safe or out. The board is nearly identical to Selchow & Richter's 1917 Home Team Baseball, the earliest version. Selchow & Richter. 12" x 14". *From the Cooper collection.*

The Major League Baseball Game, 1943. A spinner game, the advertisements in the field have patriotic messages in support of the war effort. The pocket version, also of cardboard, has pegs for players, and suggests on the envelope that it may be mailed "to service men and women overseas." G.H. Anderson, Ohio. Boxed version, 12" x 15"; pocket version, 6" x 8". *From the Cooper collection.*

Winko Baseball, 1945. A "tiddledy-wink"-type game. The plastic disc is flipped by the bat from a felt covered home plate. Where it lands on the board determines the play. Milton Bradley. 19" x 10" *From the Cooper collection.*

G.I. Joe Baseball Game, Ed Lundgren, 1946. 14" x 18". *From the Cooper collection.*

Peerless Big League Baseball, 1948. A dice controlled game using two dice to set the play. The game has an instruction book, scorecard and wooden playing pieces. Fiberboard and wood. Peerless Toy Manufacturing Co., Texas. 20" x 20". *From the Cooper collection.*

Pitch and Hit, late 1940s. A spinner game. Milton Bradley. 17" x 8". *From the Cooper collection.*

Swat Baseball, 1948. With the bat at home plate, a marble is catapulted into play by tapping the other end of the bat. The hole where it lands determines the play. Milton Bradley. 12" x 12". *From the Cooper collection.*

Play Ball: A Baseball Game of Skill, late 1940s. A marble game. The marble was shot by finger onto a field with holes. Where it rested named the play. Rosebud Art Company, New York. 12" x 8". *From the Cooper collection.*

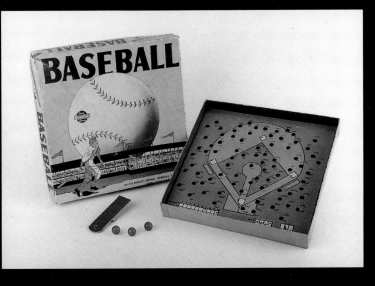

Baseball, c. late 1940s. A marble is catapulted onto a field of holes that set the play. Milton Bradley. 9" x 9". *From the Cooper collection.*

Parker Brothers Baseball Game, 1950. Cards are dealt to set the play. *From the Cooper collection.*

Beacon's Television Baseball Game, 1950s. Using the mirror and a pencil you move around the bases. If you can stay in the base path while looking at the mirror you get a home run. If you slip outside, you are out. Score is kept on the reverse. Preview-Radsell Co. 4.5" x 3". *From the Cooper collection.*

Wiry Dan's Electric Baseball Game, 1950. A battery powered game. The various spots on the field are touch by the wire, and if the light comes on the play is made. Harrett-Gilmore Inc., New York. 8" x 11". *From the Cooper collection.*

Bible Baseball, c. 1950. Though scored like real baseball, the cube is rolled to find the number of the bible question you must answer to get a hit. The questions are in a book, and the players start at page one working their way through the book page by page. Standard Publishing, Ohio. 7" x 11". *From the Cooper collection.*

Jacmar Big League Electric Baseball, c. 1952. Facsimile autographs of a number of players, including Warren Spahn, Bob Feller, Enos Slaughter, Henry Sauer, Allie Reynolds, Richie Ashburn, Robert Shantz, Monte Irvin, and Joe Black. Interestingly, Fred McKie sent me a photocopy of the box top of his game that had Ashburn's name as Artchie, apparently a mistake on the company's part. This is a spinner game. The pitcher and hitter wheels are spun. They are connected to a light, which, when on confirms the play. There was a photo sheet of all the players with facsimile autographs. Jacmar. 10" x 8". *From the Cooper collection.*

Ozark Ike's Complete 3 Game Set, 1956. A single die game. Ray Gotto the cartoonist created the popular comic strip "Ozark Ike" which ran 1955-1958. Builtrite. 11" x 6". *From the Cooper collection.*

105

Cadaco's All-Star Baseball Game

Vincent F. Hink

Cadaco's All-Star Baseball game was designed by former Major League center fielder, Ethan Allen, to reproduce realistic game results by translating a player's actual statistical performance to a cardboard player disc. The individual player discs, when placed onto a spinner device on the game board or field, would produce a variety of results such as a home run, a strike out, a double play, etc. By grouping the discs into teams, one or more players can manage an "All Star Team" of his or her choosing and play a simulated game of baseball in about twenty minutes to one-half hour.

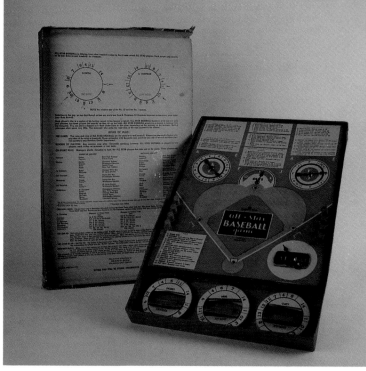

All-Star Baseball Game, 1941. This game was designed by Ethan Allen, a former major league out fielder. This is the first of a series of games issued almost annually until the present. The game board and the inside box top with the rules of play and the player disc list. The disc goes over the spinner template, and the spinner is spun to determine play. The outside spinners in the field are strategy spinners and middle spinner is an out marker. Cadaco-Ellis, Chicago. 19" x 12.5". *Courtesy of Vincent Hink.*

A 1947 photograph of Yale coach Ethan Allen and his first baseman, George Walker Bush, and Babe Ruth. This is the year that Yale went to the college world series.

Since 1941, the first year of issue, the game has gone through many variations in design, color, and size of the box, as well as the player discs. Many of these variations are illustrated in the accompanying photographs and chart. The fact that there are so many variations makes this game an attractive object for collectors. Although the game itself remains the same in terms of how it was played, the fact that each year the game was issued with a new set of player discs made each issue unique and this distinguished All-Star Baseball from other games which have been produced over an extended period of time. It would be similar to Monopoly being issued each year with a new set of properties or Community Chest cards.

For the most part it is not difficult to identify the games issued in the early years of production. The

copyrights are located on the outside and inside of the box top and also on the game board. The latest copyright of the three indicates the year of issue. Until 1952 the player discs included with each were listed of the inside of the box top. In 1953 the list was discontinued and after that year one must have a complete list of player discs from another source in order to identify the correct year of issue. At about this same time the box was changed from a blue background color to dark green. The copyrights then often remained unchanged from one year to the next. Some of the subtle design differences in the game box during this period are listed on the chart. During the period between 1946 and 1954, "Special Edition" games were issued which also included a set of "All Time Great" player discs. These games were slightly larger than the regular edition, included a stand-up scoreboard, and were packaged in a blue box, which, in the late 1940s, was changed to red.

The discs were originally produced on thick rigid cardboard. In 1946 the discs were printed on thinner stock and became much more susceptible to damage. In the mid-1950s the cardboard discs switched from gray to dark green backs. Beginning with the 1959 issue the discs once again were changed and were printed on a heavy grade paper stock. This has been

106

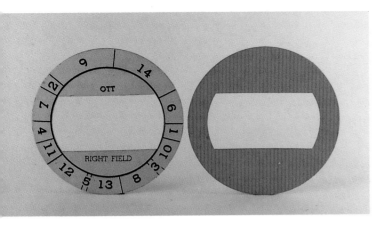

The 1941 player discs. Two things to notice: the number 1 space is offset to the right and the back is striped. *Courtesy of Vincent Hink.*

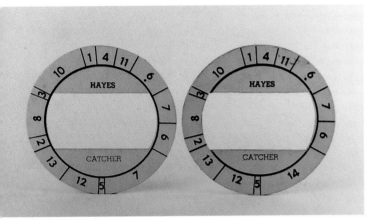

The 1942 and 1944 Hayes discs. The disc on the left is the Hayes error disc of 1942. The seven appears in two places. The error was continued in 1943, but corrected on the 1944 disc which is seen on the right. Also note the dot under the 6 to distinguish it from the 9. This innovation originated with the 1942 series. *Courtesy of Vincent Hink.*

the case ever since. After the beginning of the "paper disc" era there were almost yearly changes in the appearance of the discs. Among the most remarkable was the change of the background color of the discs from white to gray after 1962 and the elimination of the center cutout in 1969. It is also important for a collector to know that the disc sets were available by mail directly from Cadaco, so many older games have mixed sets of discs.

All Star Baseball has been issued continuously by Cadaco (now Cadaco-Rapid Mounting) between 1941 and 1993. It appears, however, that the licensing requirements that now apply to the game threaten to end over fifty years of enjoyment for baseball fans of all ages.

Ethan Allen had a multifaceted career in baseball. He began in the major leagues in 1926 with the Cincinnati Reds playing center field. He stayed with the Reds until being traded to the New York Giants in

1931. He also put in time with the St. Louis Cardinals, the Philadelphia Phillies, Chicago Cubs, and the old St. Louis Browns where he finished his playing days in 1939. After retiring as an active player with a .300 average he signed on with the National League as the Director of the League Film Bureau. During this time period he also worked on the revision of his popular baseball fundamentals book, Baseball: Major League Techniques and Tactics, which was first published by the Macmillan Company in 1938 and went through several editions. He became the baseball coach at Yale University in 1946 succeeding "Smoky Joe" Wood, and took his team, with first baseman George Bush, to the College World Series in 1947. During his college coaching career his teams won more than 300 games.

He was a graduate of the University of Cincinnati, where he played basketball, ran track, and threw the discus in addition to excelling at baseball. He received his masters degree from Columbia University in 1932 and was inducted into the Ohio Baseball Hall of Fame in 1985.

All-Star Baseball Game, 1943. The strategy spinners and out dial have been deleted. The outs are kept with pegs in the lower left of the board. There are now strategy discs that are used on the spinner template. Cadaco-Ellis, Chicago. 19" x 12.5". *Courtesy of Vincent Hink.*

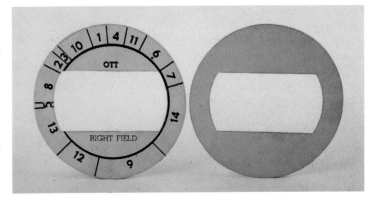

1943 player discs. The back is now white and the number 1 space is now located at top center. *Courtesy of Vincent Hink.*

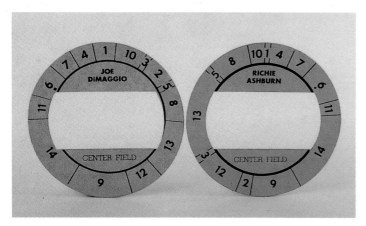

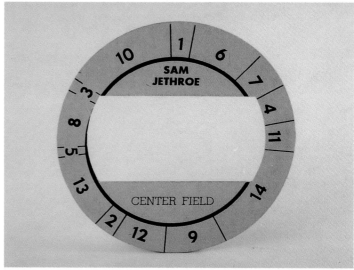

1948 and 1949 player discs. On the left is the 1948 disc, which has the number 3, 5, and 13 spaces located on the right side of the disc and the number 11 space on left side at the nine o'clock position. The 1949 discs reverses the numbers so the 11 is on the right in the three o'clock position and the 3, 5, and 13 are on the left. *Courtesy of Vincent Hink.*

1951 player disc. Sam Jethro was an early black player in the majors. The number 6 space does not have a dot under it. This is true of all the discs in the series, and is the only time it was done other than the first edition in 1941. *Courtesy of Vincent Hink.*

1943 and 1949 All-Star Baseball Games. The color of the 1949 is a different shade than the earlier game. The darker blue continued through at least 1946, and the light blue was issued by 1949 at the latest. I haven't seen any copyrighted games from the intervening years. *Courtesy of Vincent Hink.*

1950 All-Star Baseball Game, Special Edition. This 1950 special edition includes discs for the all time great players. This larger red boxed edition was in addition to the regular annual edition. It has a three dimension grandstand and a special board design. The Special Edition series was started in 1946, and was issued in a blue box. Cadaco-Ellis. 14" x 22". *Courtesy of Vincent Hink.*

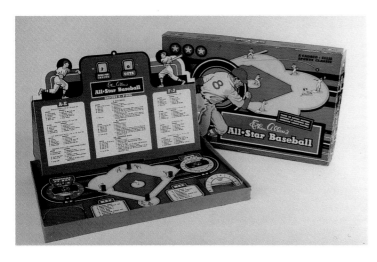

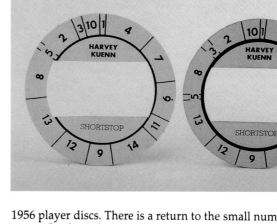

1956 player discs. There is a return to the small number 3 space. On the right is an all time great disc that began to be included in 1955. It has a heavier ring around it than the regular all star disc. *Courtesy of Vincent Hink.*

1955 All-Star Baseball Game. In 1955 the game was redesigned from the green box to the game board. There is a vertical score board and one spinner dial for each team. The reason for the additional spinner is that each one now has a defensive strategy, K-P, dial. Cadaco-Ellis. 19" x 12.5". *Courtesy of Vincent Hink.*

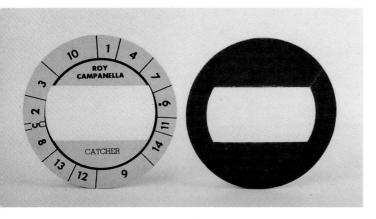

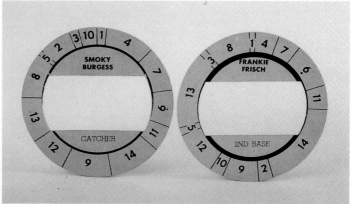

1957 and 1958 discs. On the left is the 1957 disc. Note the solid lines beside the three, compared with the broken line in the 1958 disc. The 1958 disc on the right has a heavier ring. They continue to have the green back. *Courtesy of Vincent Hink.*

1955 player discs. The number 3 space has been enlarged and the backs are now dark green. "All Time Great" discs were added to the game this year, consolidating the special edition with the regular edition. *Courtesy of Vincent Hink.*

1958 All-Star Baseball Game. Note that Ethan Allen's name is gone from the box top and the scoreboard. His name and picture do appear in the disc wells, taken out of its position for this picture. Other changes include the change of the K-P dial to a K-O dial. *Courtesy of Vincent Hink.*

109

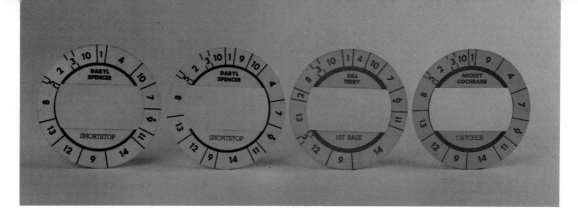

1959 and 1960 player discs. The black printed discs are regular all stars and the red printed discs are all-time greats. In 1959 the discs became paper and there are two number 10 spaces instead of one large 10 space. In 1960 they also split up the number 9 space. *Courtesy of Vincent Hink.*

1959 All-Star Baseball Game. The disc wells have disappeared, with the discs being stored under the board. We've left the score board off so you can see that storage compartment at the top of the board with the convenient hole for lifting it. Ethan Allen's name and image are in the lower right hand corner. The box top is slightly different with the Mr. Fun Spells Cadaco logo in the upper right hand corner. *Courtesy of Vincent Hink.*

1962 All-Star Baseball Game. The box top graphics have undergone a major redesign. The score board is cut differently with straighter lines. On the game board images of players are added in the infield. The discs now have a gray background for the current all stars and a red background for the all-time greats, with red centers for the outfielders and gray for the infielders. Cadaco-Ellis, 19" x 12.5". *Courtesy of Vincent Hink.*

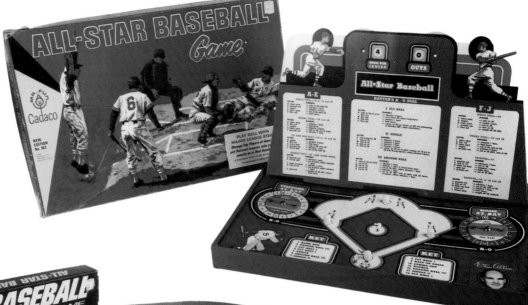

1966 All-Star Baseball Game. The box top now bears a more realistic graphic. The inside is basically the same. The gray is a lighter shade than in the previous example. This color varies from year to year, as do number placements. *Courtesy of Vincent Hink.*

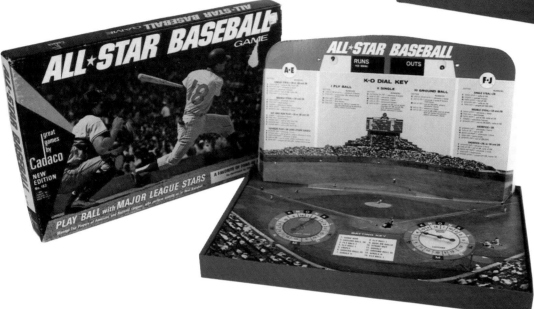

1968 All-Star Baseball Game. In 1968 the game underwent a major redesign. The graphics went to a four color photograph, inside and out. The park inside is Wrigley Field in Chicago. The discs are solid, and the spinner is mounted on a plastic sleeve into which the disc is placed. Ethan Allen still gets credit for developing the game in the box on the lower right hand corner of the box top. Cadaco Ellis is now Cadaco, Inc. 19" x 12.5". *Courtesy of Vincent Hink.*

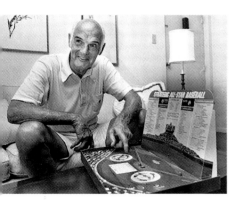

Ethan Allen with a later version of All-Star Baseball.

1968 All-Star Baseball Game. This later edition of the 1968 copyrighted game has only minor changes. This basic design continued through 1988. Ethan Allen still gets credit on the box top. *Courtesy of Vincent Hink.*

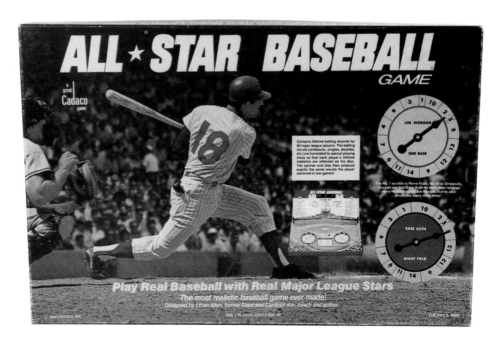

All Star Baseball
Through the Years

1941
Box Description/Copyrights. Dark blue box top with stylized baseball player (#19) on front. © 1941 on box top, outside & inside; 1941 on game board.
Discs. 40 thick, rigid, glossy white fronts, yellowish stripped back. #1 (HR) space offset at 11:00.
Remarks. First year issue, player list on inside of box top.

1942
Box Description/Copyrights. No change in box or game board. © 1942 on box top and game board.
Discs. Same as 1941, except that #1 space is centered at 12:00 and a dot now appears under the #6.
Remarks. Note that the Hayes disc has two #7 spaces. The larger space should be #14.

1943
Box Description/Copyrights. Same as 1942, except that the inside box top is now gray cardboard rather than white and the AE and FJ strategy spinners and out dial are removed. © 1943 on box top and 1942 on the board.
Discs. They now have white backs. Red and white AE and FJ strategy discs are now included.

1944
Box Description/Copyrights. Same as 1943.
Discs. Discs are slightly smaller in circumference.
Remarks. Hayes disc is corrected. The smaller discs have only been observed with the © 1943 box, but there have been 1944 games advertised for sale.

1945
Box Description/Copyrights. No changes. No games with ©1945 have been observed.
Remarks. Possibly no new edition issued.

1946
Box Description/Copyrights. Same as 1944 for regular edition. A larger blue box with a stylized player (#7) on the box top was used for a "Special Edition" with All Time Greats. ©1943 on outside box top and 1946 on the inside. ©1942 on the game board for the regular edition.
Discs. This is the first example of the thinner cardboard discs. Also, AE & FJ discs were no longer red.
Remarks. This is believed to be the first year for the Special Edition (large box) which included 20 additional All Time Great discs. This game box is slightly larger than the regular edition and has cardboard stand-up bleachers.

1947
Box Description/Copyrights. No game box with ©1947 has been observed in either regular or special editions.
Discs. A set believed to be issued in 1947 is printed on thin cardboard with a white face and gray back.
Remarks. It is possible that a 1947 issue was released in the 1946 box without an updated player list on the inside of the box top. (See 1949 remarks.)

1948
Box Description/Copyrights. The regular edition is the same as 1947. No information is available for a Special Edition.
Discs. The 1948 disc set continues to be printed on thin cardboard. There is a distinct color variation from the 1947 discs and the spaces are positioned differently.
Remarks. These discs are more of an ivory color and the #3 and #5 spaces are located at 2:00 while the #11 space is position at 9:00.

1949
Box Description/Copyrights. Lighter blue game box with ©1949 on the inside box top, 1943 on the outside, and 1942 o the game board. No information available for a Special Edition.
Discs. 1949 disc set has the #3, #5, and #13 spaces all on the left side of the discs.
Remarks. This is the first year yet observed that the color of the box has been changed to a lighter blue color. Note that no boxes have been observed for 1947 and 1948, and these could also be light blue, if they were ever issued.

1950
Box Description/Copyrights. Same as 1949 with a ©1940 on the inside box top. The Special Edition has ©1950 on the inside and ©1946 on the outside of the box top, as well as on the game board.
Discs. Discs are similar in appearance to the 1949 edition.
Remarks. No remarkable changes on the regular edition. The Special Edition now came in a red box with the same format as the 1946 blue box.

1951
Box Description/Copyrights. Same as 1950 with ©1951 on inside and outside of the box top and 1950 on the game board. No 1951 red box has been observed.
Discs. Discs are similar in appearance to the 1950 issue except that the dot under the #6 has been removed.
Remarks. This is the first change in the copyright on the outside of the box top since 1943. The dot under the #6 is removed for the first time since the 1941 issue, but only for one year.

1952

Box Description/Copyrights. No changes in appearance of the blue box editions. ©1951 on the outside and 1952 on the inside box, with 1950 on the game board. No red box has been observed.

Discs. Discs similar to previous issue except that the dot is returned under the #6.

Remarks. There were two sets of discs issued in 1952, possibly one in the spring based on 1951 statistics and another in the late fall based on 1952 stats. This probably began the period of fall issues which continued into the 1960s.

1953

Box Description/Copyrights. No changes on blue box. ©1953 on inside and outside box top, and 1950 on the game board. The red box has ©1952 on the outside, 1953 on the inside of the box top, and 1952 on the board.

Discs. Similar to 1952.

Remarks. Note that this was the first year that a list of player discs was not printed on the inside of the box top.

1954

Box Description/Copyrights. It is believed that both the blue box edition and the green box with a #8 stylized player on the top were issued with the 1954 disc set. This is the final year for the red box Special All-Time Great Edition. ©1953 on inside and outside box top, 1950 on game board, and 1952 on scoreboard. No blue box edition with ©1954 has been observed, and no green box edition with only ©1954 has been observed.

Discs. 1954 disc sets were issued with gray backs, as they had been since 1946, as well as with the new green back, which continued through 1958. The green back discs were issued with the red box Special Edition and may also have been issued in a green box later in the year.

Remarks. This appears to be a transition year from the original blue box game with one disc spinner, to the newly designed green box game. The green box game had a stand up score board and two spinners for the discs and implemented the new defensive feature of the game (K-P dial). Also the cardboard discs were issued with two different color backs for the only time.

1955

Box Description/Copyrights. All games now are issued in the new green box. The copyrights are 1955 on the outside and 1954 on the nside of the box top, with 1955 on the scoreboard and the game board.

Discs. The disc set is comprised of 40 regular players with a set of 20 All Time Greats. They have dark green backs and are distinguishable by an enlarged #3 space for this year only.

Remarks. This game was the first to use the defensive feature (K-P dial). There are examples of game boards with one disc storage well and also with two.

1956

Box Description/Copyrights. Same as 1955. No games have been observed with a 1956 copyright.

Discs. The new 1956 disc set returned the #3 space to its previous size.

Remarks. Minor changes on game board.

1957

Box Description/Copyrights. Same a previous green box games. ©1957 on outside and inside of box top and scoreboard. The game board is ©1955.

Discs. The new 1957 disc set is basically similar to 1956.

Remarks. The offensive feature was modified as the K-P dial was changed to a K-O dial. This change has continued to the present.

1958

Box Description/Copyrights. No changes in the game box from 1957. No 1958 copyrighted games have been observed.

Discs. 1958 disc set is similar to 1957. The discs continued to be made of cardboard stock with dark green backs. 1958 discs have been observed, however, printed on heavy paper with white backs.

Remarks. This is the final year for cardboard discs. The 1958 discs which were printed on paper were probably issued late in the year, before the new 1959 set was released.

1959-1961

Box Description/Copyrights. During this three year period the game continued to be issued in the familiar green box. The copyrights were 1959 and 1960 on the game box, while the game board and scoreboards continued to keep the 1955 and 1957 copyrights.

Discs. The 1959 disc set was the first to be exclusively issued on heavy paper. The regular player discs were printed in black on white paper while the All Time Great discs were printed in red. There were four sets of white paper player discs during this period.

Remarks. With the introduction of paper discs, the #10 (strikeout) space was divided into two spaces for most players. This was expanded the following year to include the #9 space (walk) and has continued to the present time.

1962-1969

Box Description/Copyrights. During this seven year period the game box was changed several times. The familiar dark green box changed to a lighter shade of green and the design of the box top was changed. Notable copyrights are 1962 and

1966 on the inside of the box top.

Discs. In 1962 the player discs were issued on gray paper with black print and lines. Over the next several years the discs would have many changes from year to year, including background colors, print colors and the texture or finish of the paper. Print size and thickness would vary as well. The All Time Great discs were printed on red background paper with various color inks.

Remarks. During this period of time it became common for more than one set of discs to be issued during the year.

1969

Box Description/Copyrights. The game box was redesigned. The box top was now a photo representation. The copyright on the box is 1968, and remained so until 1988.

Discs. The disc set continued to be issued on gray paper background. The number of discs changed to 60 regular players. The All Time Great discs were no longer included.

Remarks. The 1968 edition began a new era. The game box that year remained essentially unchanged until 1989. During this time many changes were made to the discs, most notably the elimination of the center cut out and the corresponding change to the spinners. Another variation included the two year experiment with a divided #1 space. Also, in the early eighties, it was common for an "A" and a "B" set of cards to be issued.

1989

Box Description/Copyrights. The game box was redesigned significantly for the first time since 1968. The box is now red in color with a square shape that, at 2 inches, is deeper than previous issues. The copyright changed and the discs and playing field are greatly changed.

Discs. The discs are now issued with the player's picture in the center. The copyright and MLPA logo appear on the disc. The discs have a yellow background and the reverse has player statistics for five previous years and lifetime totals.

Remarks. This is the most drastic redesign of the box and discs since the game began in 1941. The game was issued in this format in 1989, 1990, 1991, and 1993. Cadaco reportedly will not issue a new edition in 1994 and future editions are questionable.

Chapter 8

20th Century Card Games

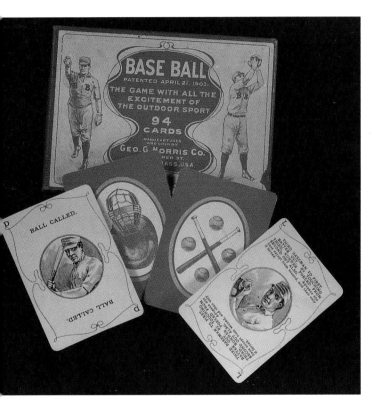

Fan Craze (WG2), 1904. A deck of 54 cards with photos of stars from the National League. the American League deck is known bycollectors as WG3, has 51 cards and was manufactured in 1906. The American League has blue backs and the National League has red backs. In addition to the name and team of the player, there is a game situation on each card. Fan Craze Company, Cincinnati. 3.5" x 2.5". *From the Cooper collection.*

Base Ball, 1903. A deck of 94 cards sets the plays. Geo. G. Norris Co. *Courtesy of Mike Brown.*

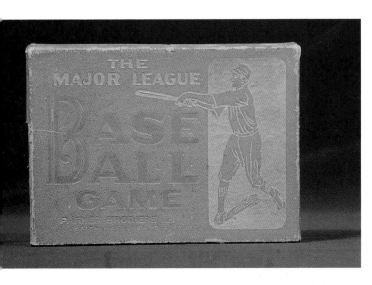

The Major League Base Ball Game, early 1900s. Inside are lithographed generic baseball cards with either red or blue backs. Each card is marked with a specific action. 4" x 5". Parker Brothers. *Courtesy of Marty and Debby Krim.*

Game of Batter Up, 1908. The box bottom has a playing field, where discs are used as players. There are 16 different situation cards, for the "Batted Ball." Fenner Game Co., Toledo, Ohio. Box: 3.5" x 5.5". *From the Cooper collection.*

The American National Game Baseball, 1909. American National Game Co., Uhrichsville, Ohio. *Courtesy of Mike Brown.*

Baseballitis, 1909. The box top of the this card game has a cartoon with the players talking it up. "Bonehead can't hit it" says the shortstop. "Git 'em on de jump," pipes in the second baseman. The cards have similar Damon Runyan-type phraseology. For a two-bagger the catcher says "First time he ever done it." The hitter responds "How's dat fer de cream?" Baseballitis Card Co., Milwaukee. Box: 5.5" x 4". *From the Cooper collection.*

Jake Aydelott
Games: 14
Wins: 5
Losses: 9
Pct.: .357
ERA: 4.79

The Field to the Parlor: The Aydelott's Base Ball Cards, 1910. In a history of baseball card games of 1885 Aydelott's game is mentioned. This one is patented in 1910, and one can only wonder why it took so long to patent. Aydelott was a 19th century professional player. The game has 125 cards with various playing situations, a paper field, and wooden pawns as base runners. Aydelott's Base Ball Card Company, Detroit. 4.5" x 3". A recent find makes this game relatively common. *From the Cooper collection.*

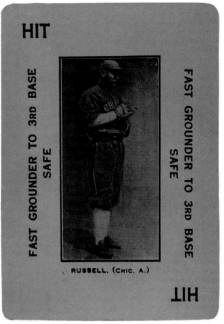

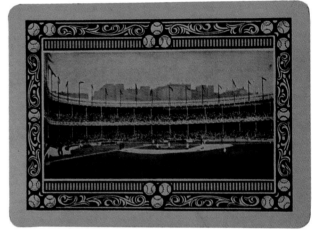

Polo Grounds Playing Cards (WG4), c. 1910. A complete set of 52 cards has a sepia-toned full-body pose of a major league player. Thirty different players are pictured, and some are featured more than once. The back has a picture of the Polo Grounds in New York. Manufacturer unknown. 3.5" x 2.5". *From the Cooper collection.*

Left: The Great National Game of Base Ball, 1910. Made in Germany, the cards have line drawings of either a pitcher, a fielder, a batter, or a catcher. Cards are dealt and players turn up their cards one at a time. When the cards match, the player who yells "snap" first gets the card and all the cards under it. Manufacturer unknown. 2" x 3". Right: Snap, 1910. Played as the game on the left, it measures only 1" x 2". *From the Cooper collection.*

117

Napoleon LaJoie Baseball Game, 1913. The cards have LaJoie on the back. We have the cards, the instructions, and the game board. The game box is the same as the National American Baseball Game by Parker Brothers seen at the bottom of page 123, but it does not have a divider. Parker Brothers. Folded game board size: 5" x 3.5". *From the Cooper collection.*

The National Game (WG5), c. 1913. A complete set of 54 cards with photographs of 43 identified players, 9 action cards, and two cards for scoring and rules. National Base Ball Playing Card Company, Massachusetts. 2.5" x 3.5". *From the Cooper collection.*

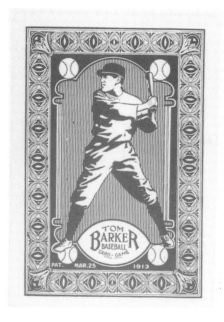

Tom Barker's Baseball Card Game (WG6), 1913. The player images on this deck that also appear on The National Game deck (WG5) are exactly the same, though there are different players included in this deck. The cards have a different back. Tom Barker Game Company. 2.5" x 3.5". *From the Cooper collection.*

New Card Baseball Game, 1920. The National Card Baseball Co., Springfield, Ohio. *Courtesy of Mike Brown.*

Hatfield's Parlor Base-Ball Game, 1914. The game has sixty cards, 12 discs and a folding playing field. Hatfield Company, Chicago. Box: 8.5" x 6". *From the Cooper collection.*

Baseball Game, 1917. "No Kings-No Queens-No Jacks" in this World War I era baseball card game. The cards have team names of the era. Most known sets in this commonly found game are in nearly pristine condition, leading one to conclude that they are either a warehouse find or a reproduction. Manufacturer unknown. Size: 3.5" x 2.5". *From the Cooper collection.*

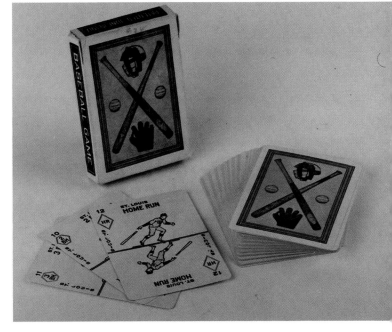

The Great Mails Baseball Card Game (WG7), c. 1920. A set of 56 cards invented by George Groves of California, and published by the Great Walter Mails Base Ball Game Co., Santa Monica, California. The deck is marked "endorsed by Major League Players" and "55 Big League Photos." Each photo card has the players name in block letters and a facsimile autograph. The set includes the Pacific Coast League, Minor League, Major League and Walter Mails himself. 2.5" x 3.25". *Courtesy of Marty & Debby Krim.*

Psychic Base Ball Game, 1926. This is the earliest version of the game. It used cards to create the play, and had no board, though it did come with a score card. It originally cost 75 cents. Psychic Base Ball Corp. 3" x 4". *From the Cooper collection.*

Psychic Base Ball Game, 1927. The cards are the same, but the box top has playing field with holes for pegs to be used as runners. This version cost $1. Psychic Base Ball Corp. 4.5" x 3". *From the Cooper collection.*

Psychic Base Ball Game, 1935. This was the latest version of the card game and came with a board. The cards remained unchanged. Parker Brothers had apparently purchased the game from Psychic Base Ball Corp. and remarketed it. Parker Brothers. 16" x 10". *From the Cooper collection.*

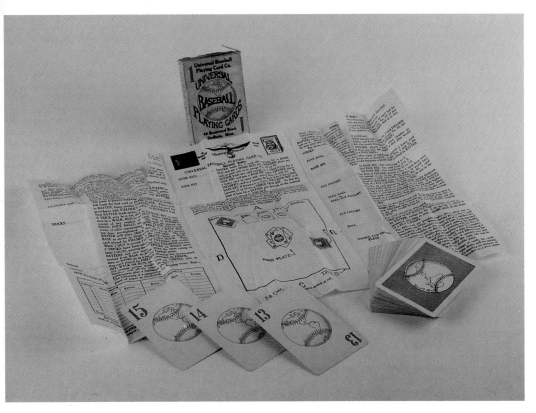

Universal Baseball Playing Cards, 1927. Various batter and fielder cards establish the play. It is almost like the contemporary game of Uno. Universal Baseball Playing Card Co., Dedham, Massachusetts. 2.5" x 3.5". *From the Cooper collection.*

The National Game: A Baseball Card Game (WG8), 1936. 52 cards with pictures of 52 major league players and situations, came with card board playing field and wooden players. Blank backs. In addition to this version, it also came in a larger version. S&S Games Company. 5" x 4.25". *From the Cooper collection.*

Big League Base Ball Card Game, 1933. Made up of offensive and defensive cards. Whitman Publishing. Box: 3.5" x 5". *From the Cooper collection.*

Fan Ball, 1936. Cards establish the play on a felt playing field with player discs. Fan Ball Company, Indiana. Box: 6" x 4". *From the Cooper collection.*

Star Baseball Game, 1941. Wm. P. Ulrich, Spokane, Washington. *Courtesy of Mike Brown.*

Advertising deck of card, late 1940s. Apparitions of Lou Gehrig (shown here), Babe Ruth, and Ty Cobb appear behind children playing ball on the backs of this standard deck of cards. Brown & Bigelow, St. Paul, Minnesota. 2.25" x 3.5". *From the Cooper collection.*

Base Hit, 1944. Forty cards and 18 metal men make up this game. Connie Mack endorsed the game saying, "Base Hit is real base ball played at home. That's why it is a sure hit with me, and I highly recommend it to young and old." The board is missing. Games Inc., New York. Box size: 8" x 7". *From the Cooper collection.*

Earl Gillespie Baseball Game, 1961. Earl Gillespie was a radio announcer for the Atlanta. The cards set the situation. Wei-gill Inc. Box: 3.5" x 4.5". *From the Cooper collection.*

The National American Base Ball Game., date unknown. 12 possible plays represented by cards. The same box as the Napoleon LaJoie game (page 118), but with a divider. Parker Brothers. 4" x 5.5". *From the Cooper collection.*

123

Ideal Baseball Game, 1903. Fiber board, wood, and net pockets. Karrom-Archarena, Ludington, Michigan. 29" x 29". *From the Cooper collection.*

National Base Ball Game, 1908. Lithographed tin with a contoured field. This predates the Mather's game, with the pitched ball coming down the groove and the mechanical bat hitting it. Manufacturer unknown. 18" x 23". *From the Cooper collection.*

Edward's Big League Table Base Ball Game, Edward's Manufacturing Co., Cincinnati, c. 1905. The most sophisticated of all action games. The pitcher pitches a ball in the air, and the batter attempts to hit it. There are nine total fielders with maroon uniforms, eight of whom have nets to make the putout. The knob behind home plate moves the runners around the bases in a chain driven mechanism. Wood, metal and felt, with leatherette covering the sides. Manufacturer unnown. 27" x 27". *From the Cooper collection.*

Mather's Parlor Base Ball Game, 1909. One ball acts as the pitched ball, the other as the runner, moving in the grooves of the base path. The board is contoured to direct the ball. Lithographed tin. Mathers, Canton, Ohio. 18" x 24". *From the Cooper collection.*

MATHER'S PARLOR BASE BALL GAME

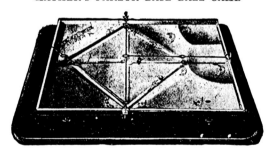

No.	Per doz.
1043 Mather's Parlor Base Ball Game, a perfect reproduction of base ball, plays all the features, constructed of metal, size 19x23, based on the laws of gravitation, National League rules, two or more players.................	**$48 00**

Advertisement for Mather's Parlor Base Ball Game in the A.C. McClurg catalog, 1908-1909.

Home Run, 1920s. A double shooter lithographed tin pinball-type game. Each player takes a side. Manufacturer unknown. 8" x 19". *From the Cooper collection.*

Junior Base Ball Game, 1913. A ball is hit in the groove of this ruler and its final location sets the play. "Interesting to both boys and girls." Benjamin-Sellar Manufacturer, Chicago. 18" x 2" *From the Cooper collection.*

Baker's Ball Game for Men and Boys, 1920. Along the wall are Cincinnati players, probably due to the proximity of Kentucky to Cincinnati and of the Reds having won the 1919 World Series. W.J. Baker Company, Newport, Kentucky. 27" x 27". *From the Cooper collection.*

TedToy-lers Base Ball Game, c. early 1920s. This wood and cardboard folding game involves having the ball pitched and swinging at it with a spring loaded bat. The fielders can scoop up the ball. The resting place of the ball sets the play. The TedToy-lers, Massachusetts. 30" x 30" board, open. *From the Cooper collection.*

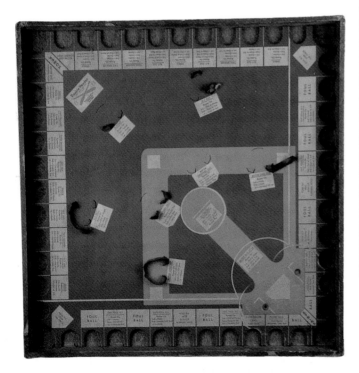

Realistic Baseball, 1925. The ball is pitched by rolling it, and the bat is finger driven. The ball may be caught by a player for an out, or roll to the wall to be put in play. Cardboard with tin players and a metal bat. Realistic Games, Patterson, New Jersey. 18" x 18". *From the Cooper collection.*

Double Header, 1920s. The ball is pitched and hit with a bat. Wood, cardboard, and paper. Redledge Manufacturing Company. 25" x 25". *From the Cooper collection.*

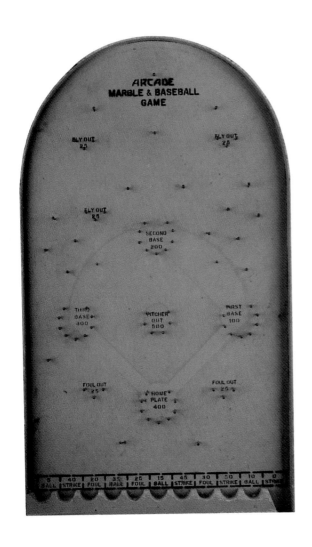

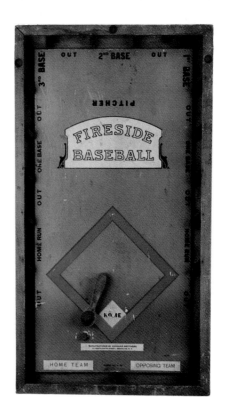

Fireside Baseball, 1927. Wood and particle board game with a spring action bat hitting a rolled ball. Schauer Brothers, New York. 15" x 26". *From the Cooper collection.*

Arcade Marble & Baseball Game, 1926. This wood and metal bagatelle game uses marbles. Another version of this game has a drawing in center field of a Babe Ruth type figure. Arcade Manufacturing Company. 24" x 12". *From the Cooper collection.*

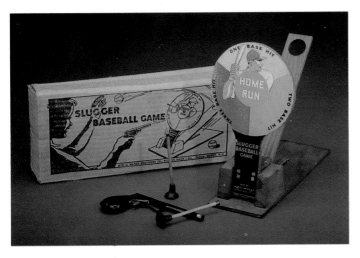

Slugger Baseball Game. Marks Brothers, Boston, Massachusetts. The ball is held on a spring loaded arm. If the target is hit with the dart, the arm is released, sending the ball toward the shooter. Comes boxed with the target, a pressed tin gun embossed with Marks, darts, and a ball. 11" x 11". *From the Cooper collection.*

Batter Up! 1929. A tin bagatelle. Joseph Schneider. 6" x 10". *From the Cooper collection.*

Home Run King, c. late 1930s. Tin wind up toy. The ball comes up through the tee and the batter hits it as he turns on a pedestal. Selrite Products Inc. 7" x 5" box. *From the Cooper collection.*

Home Run Babe, c. late 1920s. Exceedingly rare earlier version of the game, this "Babe" version is string driven. The batter turns at the waist. Selrite Products. 7" x 5". *From the Cooper collection.*

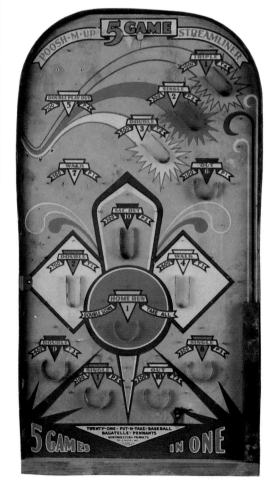

Poosh-M-Up 5 Game Streamliner, early 1930s. An early version of the Poosh-M-Up bagatelles. Tin and wood. Northwestern Products. 12" x 22". *From the Cooper collection.*

130

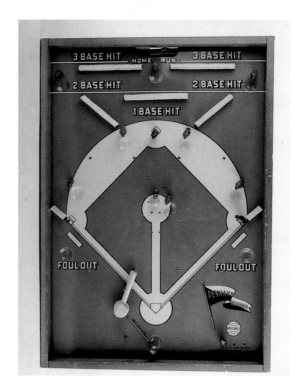

"Mac" Baseball Game, c. mid-1930s. The lever drives the ball up the pole. Where it stops sets the play. The arrows on the board keep track of the score. Lithographed tin. McDowell Manufacturing Co., Pittsburgh. 14" x 11". *From the Cooper collection.*

Pinch Hitter, 1938. Pinball type bagatelle. When the ball is hit, it moves to the round infield which is mechanically spun around. J&S Corporation, 24" x 12". *From the Cooper collection.*

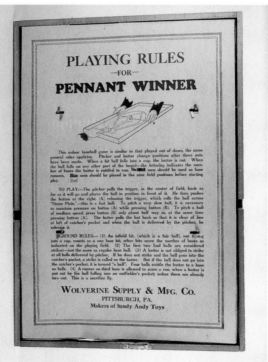

Pennant Winner, c. 1939. an extremely interesting game. There are trigger devices on the side that allow the pitcher to pitch slow, fast, or curve balls. The spring loaded bat hits the ball and it destination on the field calls the play. I've never had a game that had such an outpouring of emotional response for the game. An editorial in the New York Times by William Zinnser was devoted entirely to this childhood game, though he could not remember the name of it. He ends the piece saying, "I can't remember whether the game had a name-I like to think it was 'Baseball' - or who its manufacturer was. But in the mists of memory I see the word WOLVERINE. What "Rosebud" was to Citizen Kane, "Wolverine" is to me." This wood and metal game came in a generic cardboard box. Wolverine Supply and Manufacturing Company (also manufactured by Sandy Andy). 26" x 18". *From the Cooper collection.*

Name Unknown, c. late 1930s. Wood and felt board with spring loaded shooter and hand-powered bat device. The ball is shot to a metal clasp which determines the outcome. United Industries, Cleveland. 25" x 25". *From the Cooper collection.*

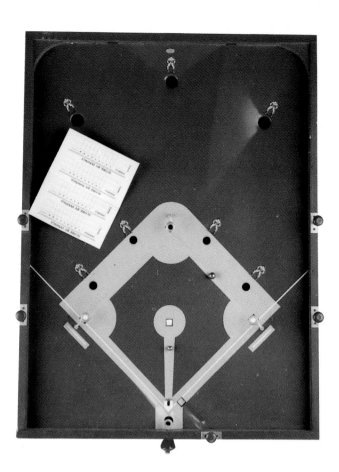

Alexander's Baseball Game, late 1930s. Wood with a contoured tin playing field. A small ball is pitched and a larger ball represents the runners and moves along grooves in the base paths. It comes in a cardboard playing box. Manufacturer unknown. 26" x 19" *From the Cooper collection.*

Dart Ball, late 1930s. The offensive play is determine by spinning the ball. The defensive play is made by throwing a suction dart at the board. Wolverine Supply Co. 20" x 20". *From the Cooper collection.*

Skor-It, late 1930s. Bagatelle of tin and glass. Northwestern Products, St. Louis. 10" x 17". *From the Cooper collection.*

Major League Baseball, 1940s. Magnetic dart board. Pressman Toy Co. 14" x 18". *From the Cooper collection.*

Lindstrom's Baseball, late 1930s. All tin bagatelle, with the back of the game being a football field. Lindstrom. 9" x 15". *From the Cooper collection.*

Pro Baseball, c. early 1940s. The ball are put into slots in the grandstand, the wheel is spun and the player hits the bat handle for in-curve, straight fast, or out-carve, releasing the ball onto the spinning wheel. Where it land determines the play. Particle board and hard rubber. Manufacturer unknown. 8.5" x 8.5". *From the Cooper collection.*

Base Ball Game, mid-1940s. Plastic and tin pinball game. Japan. 4" x 7". *From the Cooper collection.*

Bat-R-Up, late 1940s. Wooden action game, a ball is hit off the tee to go into a hole on the board. Manufacturer unknown. 15" x 15". *From the Cooper collection.*

Poosh-M-Up Big Five, late 1940s. Bagatelle game with shooter, made of glass, wood, and tin. Northwestern Products, St. Louis. 13" x 24". *From the Cooper collection.*

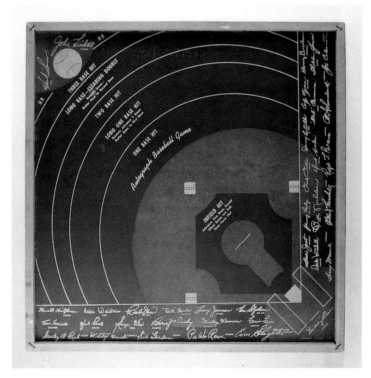

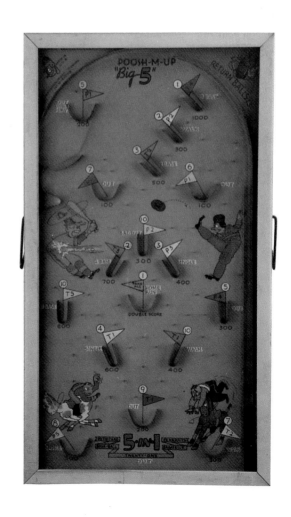

Autograph Baseball Game, 1948. A disc is flicked with a finger, and where it lands determines the play. The board has over 40 facsimile autographs of the stars of the era. F.J. Raff. 23" x 23". *From the Cooper collection.*

Poosh-M-Up Jr. 4-in-1, late 1940s. Smaller version of the Big Five. Northwestern Products, St. Louis. 11" x 18". *From the Cooper collection.*

Magnetic Dart Boards, late 1940s. American Doll Carriage and Toy Company. 13" x 15". *From the Cooper collection.*

Sport-O-Rama, 1950s. Pinball game with a device to keep track of base positions. Pin-Bo. 6.5" x 6.5". *From the Cooper collection.*

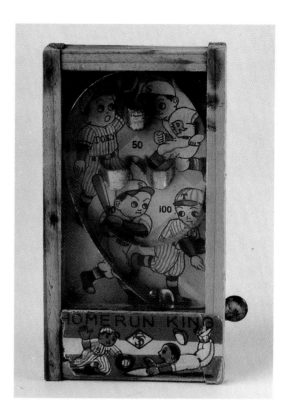

Homerun King. Pocket-sized pinball machine. Wood, tin and glass. Made in Japan. 2.5" x 4". *From the Cooper collection.*

Pinball Game, 1950s.. Tin and glass pinball game made in Japan. Manufacturer unknown. 4" x 7". *From the Cooper collection.*

All Stars Mr. Baseball Jr., 1960s. Following the tradition of the earlier games, Home Run King and Home Run Babe, this mechanical tin toy incorporates an automatic batting machine, and is battery driven. The box was part of the game. Where the ball hit the box determined the play. The seven is supposed to represent Mickey Mantle. Made in Japan. *From the Cooper collection.*

Chapter 10

20th Century Coin-Operated Games

Baseball and the Coin-Operated Machine
William E. Howard

Along with card playing and horse racing, the grand old game of baseball stands out among the most popular themes employed by coin-operated machines during the most fertile period of their history, between 1880 and the mid-1900s.

The development of coin-operated machines began amid the depression of the 1880s. Meeting public acceptance, they grew in number and variety, principally in the form of single reel machines.

Although the games employed many ingenious mechanical techniques and designs, few patents were awarded because of a legal restriction barring patents for gambling devices. The first successful patent application was J.D. Latimer's in 1893. By calling his invention a toy, he bypassed the legal prohibition. The marquee of his game reads "Game of Skill Amusement Toy." The labeling charade continues:

> "This machine not being a game of chance, we have secured a patent on it as a game of skill. Therefore, it is the only lawful device of its kind and is permitted everywhere while others have been prohibited."

How J.D. Latimer sold this nonsense to the U.S. Patent Office is a wonder. In any event, it marked the beginning of a continuous attempt to disguise coin-operated gambling machins as something other than what so many of them really were.

A 3-for-1 John A. Seamon and Co. slot machine manufactured in 1893, believed to be the first mass produced slot machine. *Courtesy of William Howard.*

An example of the popular one reel variety is this 1896 Schall Star. *Courtesy of William Howard.*

The 1893 Latimer machine, a "Game of Skill Amusement Toy." *Courtesy of William Howard.*

The 1927 Play Ball Vender. *Courtesy of William Howard.*

Advertisement for the Play Ball Vender and the Batter-Up Ball Gum Vender, both by Exhibit Supply Company.

Even when certain machines, like the *Latimer*, did manage to sneak their way past the U.S. Patent Office, it did not protect them from being copied. In 1927 *The Play Ball Vendor* was successfully patented. In 1932 B & M Products came out with a machine that was obviously copied, using virtually the same scheme and mechanism. It was called the *B & M Ball Gum* machine.

Coin-operated machines often have been categorized by collectors into four general types: slot machines, trade stimulators, vending machines, and arcade games. A slot machine is classified as one that pays off by itself, without the assistance of the ma-

chine operator. Other machines either have no obvious reward or require the machine operator to pay the player whatever reward they have won. Trade stimulators were designed primarily to do just that in small, competitive general stores of their day. Their presence stimulated customer traffic or trade into the store by offering clever machines that attracted attention and gave merchandise credits to winners. Vending machines are those that accept coins to vend merchandise to a customer, without the action of a clerk. They were often referred to as "silent salesmen." Arcade games had as their primary feature the play-

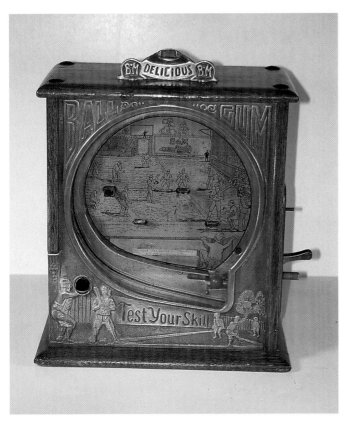

The 1932 B & M Ball Gum machine, owing much to the earlier Play Ball Vender. *Courtesy of William Howard.*

the reels had numbers in alternate shades of green and red. Roulette!

This is but one example of the never ending battle of wits between the game manufacturer, who desperately sought to keep one step ahead of the law, and the local constable in the territory in which the machine was used. When examining a machine manufactured in the 1920s or 1930s it is important to remember that the main purpose of the machine was to get your change. One of the best ways to do this is gambling, so there is a good bet that somewhere in the machine you are examining is, among other things, a gambling device.

Baseball was a natural theme for coin-operated machines. One of the earliest and most sought after examples of its use is the 1908 *Caille Baseball* trade stimulator, a revamp of the *Caille Tiger*. It paid out a token after ringing a bell and awarded various merchandise credits if the particular base hit matched the player's selection.

The 1908 Caille Baseball trade stimulator. *Courtesy of William Howard.*

ing of an amusement for the price of a coin. A fifth category, similar to the arcade games, is that of pinball machines, essentially coin operated bagatelles.

What is confusing about compartmentalizing coin-operating machines is that they often overlap. What appears to be a simple, innocent vending machine or arcade game is, in reality, an excuse to gamble. Beneath the mint vending machine or the arcade game with the strange handle lies what, in essence, is a slot machine. One of the most popular ways to disguise slot machines between 1929 and 1940 was to cover their fronts with a baseball game motif in order to confuse the local constable.

Because of all the deliberate confusion created by the manufacturers of these devices, the use of old advertisements to identify the theme and condition of these machines is critically important to collectors. If one were to look at the 1927 game of *Little Gypsy*, they would see a machine that offered a gum ball and a fortune for a coin. The advertisement that appeared int he October, 1927 issue of *Automatic Age*, a trade journal, paints quite a different picture. It describes the game having "four large cloth layouts, standard roulette wheel number 1 to 36 and double 00 with fortune on each color, and six large balls in colors on the reel, each paying 5 for 1." After reading the copy, it is easier to understand why the machine took any coin, which it hung for display in a window, and why

The development of the gum ball after the turn of the century brought about many baseball machines that offered the player at least a gum ball for his money. Perhaps the greatest influence in the popularity of baseball coin-ops was the fame of George Herman Ruth. He did the same for the coin-machine industry that he did for the Yankee Stadium, "the house that Ruth built." An advertisement in the April 19, 1930 issue of *Billboard Magazine* demonstrates the importance of Ruth and baseball in the promotion of these machines. The headline reads: "Babe Ruth signed for $80,000. How About You?" The *Champion Speed Tester* features a wonderful facial view of the Babe and another prominent athlete by inviting the player to deposit a coin and test his hand eye coordination.

An advertisement from *Billboard*, April 19, 1930, for the Big League gum ball dispenser. It uses Ruth's signing as a come-on, though he had nothing to do with the nickel gum ball machine.

The Champion Speed Tester, featuring Babe Ruth and another prominent athlete. *Courtesy of William Howard.*

The influence of baseball on coin-operated machines reached the point where baseball symbols and themes were put on the machine even when they had nothing to do with its operation. The *Little Dream Gum Machine* for Adams Gum and the *Superior Confection* machine, 1929, a slot-type gum ball machine, are two examples of this trend.

By the early 1930s examples of baseball coin-operated games depicting part of the actual game had become numerous. Perhaps the crown prince of these table model ball games was the 1931 *Hercules Midget Baseball Machine*. It pretty much wiped out the competition of its day.

Little Dream Gum Machine for Adams Gum. *Courtesy of William Howard.*

As is true of so many other forms of baseball memorabilia, the graphics of coin-operated baseball machines can be critically important to the value and desirability of a piece to the collector. The beauty of the Peo 1931 World Champion Miniature Baseball game is easy to see. Unfortunately many of the examples seen today are missing the graphics on the sides, due to the refinisher's zeal. Look for the best example you can find. By the way, later examples had a battery that allowed a light to illuminate which bases were being occupied.

An advertisement for Peo's early Play Ball game. The copy tells us that it held 2500 gum balls took 10 seconds to play. That meant five plays per minute, bringing the owner 5 cents. Besides, it says, this machine "will attract attention from 50 feet."

The Hercules Midget Baseball Game, 1931. Hercules Novelty Co., Chicago. *Courtesy of William Howard.*

Superior Confection gum ball slot machine. *Courtesy of William Howard.*

The 1931 Peo World Champion Miniature Baseball with the complete graphics intact.

While some coin-operated machines have become quite scarce, many examples remain plentiful enough to be accessible to collectors...and new examples, previously unknown, are still turning up. That's what is really fun! So good luck to all who join the hunt.

Slot Machines

The Pace Baseball Vendor slot machine. This beautiful machine has a cast iron front. *Courtesy of William Howard.*

Mills five cent slot machine, with original marquee, delayed payout and a mint dispenser. Mills Novelty Co., Chicago. 1930s. *Courtesy of Mike Brown.*

Trade Stimulators

The trade stimulator is exemplified by the Exhibit Supply Play Ball penny drop, where pennies not gobbled up in the play field landed in base hit slots that were rewarded with money or merchandise credit. Also, the Jennings Grandstand Baseball variation paid out one, two, three, or four tokens worth 25 cents each if singles, doubles, triples, or homers lined up on a three machine played with a nickel. Similarly, the Hi Fly Machine rewarded the player with money or merchandise for a successful flip of the nickel or combination of nickels. Many of these machines now rest at the bottom of the Pacific Ocean near Los Angeles, thanks to the zealous efforts of a Prosecuting Attorney named Earl Warren, who later became Chief Justice of The Supreme Court.

Millard's Miniature Baseball advertisement. The penny was hit like a baseball, and where it fell determined the score. The copy reads in part, "Draws and holds crowds like a magnet...It is nothing unusual for this marvelous money-maker to take in $100 a week when prominently displayed. *Courtesy of Phill Emmert.*

143

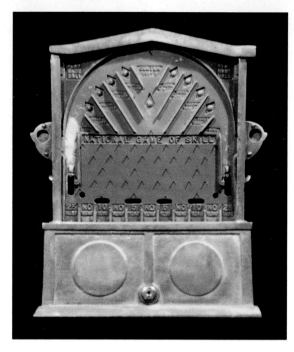

National Game of Skill. One cent penny flip for two players similar to the Exhibit Supply Play Ball. 1930s. *Courtesy of Mike Brown.*

New National Machines

The National Base Ball machine is released. The Base Ball machine can be operated with or without prizes. Either way operated it earns astonishing profits.

NATIONAL COLLAPSIBLE STAND

Standard in size and height for either Mills or Jennings machines. Folds up like a jack-knife. Set us in 30 seconds, only two small screws necessary. All parts fastened together with square rivets and all joints spot welded. We guarantee this stand to endure the roughest treatment.

An advertisement for Base Ball. Though similar to the Exhibit Supply Play Ball, this is a different game, and is rare.

Play Ball. Exhibit Supply Company, Chicago. 18" x 9". *From the Cooper collection.*

Miniature Baseball: World Champion. The machine on the left is an early version, dated early 1930s. It has no decal on the side. The newer version, early 1940s, has a light at each base that automatically shows which base the runner is on. Peo. 18" x 9". *From the Cooper collection.*

Jennings Grandstand five-cent trade stimulator. A slot machine that dispenses tokens to the winners. These could be turned in for cash. Late 1920s. *Courtesy of William Howard.*

Marvel's Pop-Up, 1930s. Marvel Manufacturing. 20" x 12". *From the Cooper collection.*

Hi-Fly baseball machine. *Courtesy of William Howard.*

Base Ball: Game of Skill. The ball was hit for the batting device in the upper right hand corner of the machine. The slot it fell into determined the runs or points. While the label reads "No Gambling," this was in fact a gambling device. 20" x 15". *From the Cooper collection.*

Pace Perfection Spiral Baseball, 1931. With aluminum scoring marquee. Pace Mfg. Co., Chicago, Illinois. *Courtesy of Mike Brown.*

Name unknown, c. late 1940s. This is a gum ball-like arcade game. Manufacturer unknown. 14" x 9". *From the Cooper collection.*

Pick Your Sluggers, 1931. Initially made as a golf machine called "Barnyard Golf," the paper was changed for baseball, with images of various stars. Peo Manufacturing. *Courtesy of Mike Brown.*

Baseball, 1920s. Early pneumatically operated spiral baseball machine. Manufacturer unknown. *Courtesy of Mike Brown.*

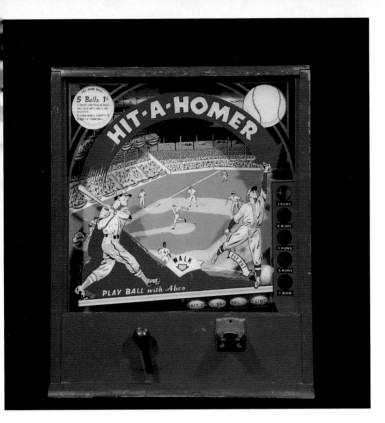

Hit-A-Homer. Tabletop arcade game from the 1940s. *Courtesy of Mike Brown.*

Vending Machines

Some vending machines doubled as games, like *Play Baseball*, which challenged the player with how many runs he could register with his gum ball. Victor Vending Baseball featured the logos of many of the early major league teams on the glass.

Play Baseball vending machine. The Kholm Co. *Courtesy of William Howard.*

Hit A Homer coin-op. Late 1930s to early 1940s. *From the Cooper collection.*

Victor Vending Baseball gum vendor. *Courtesy of William Howard.*

Play Ball! Gum dispenser game. Leaf, 1950s. *Courtesy of Mike Brown.*

Early baseball pinball machine that dispensed gum balls to the winners. C. 1930s. *Courtesy of Mike Brown.*

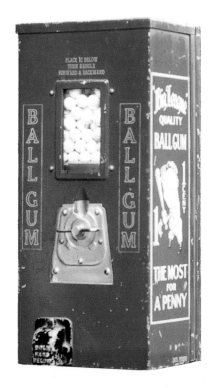

Big League Ball Gum, 1923. Advance Machine Co., Chicago, Illinois. *Courtesy of Mike Brown.*

Arcade Games

This is probably the most plentiful area of coin-operated machines, but, again, the gambling and trade stimulator features of this games must be seen "between the lines." On close inspection, the counter top version of the Atlas Indicator Works baseball game discloses that, in reality, it is a pure gambling device, rewarding only home runs that remain displayed behind the glass until the player is paid off. Many arcade games incorporated the feature of returning the player's coin if he was successful, as seen in the cast iron *Bat-a-Peny,* 1926.

Atlas Indicator Works Baseball game, floor version. *Courtesy of William Howard.*

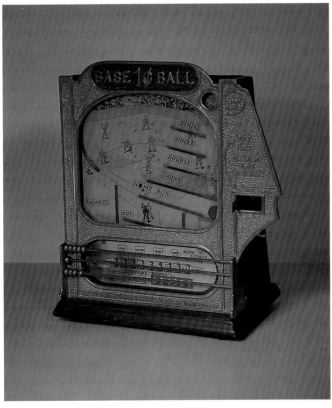

Atlas Indicator Works Baseball game, counter top version. *Courtesy of William Howard.*

Three strikes for a penny in this mechanical coin-op, c. 1900. Blackburn Manufacturing Co., San Antonio, Texas. *Courtesy of Mike Brown..*

149

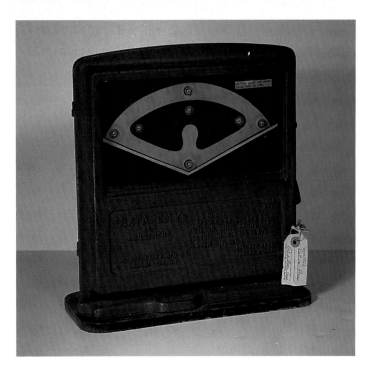

Bat-A-Peny, 1926. Cast iron machine by the Bat-A-Peny Corporation, Rochester, New York. *Courtesy of William Howard.*

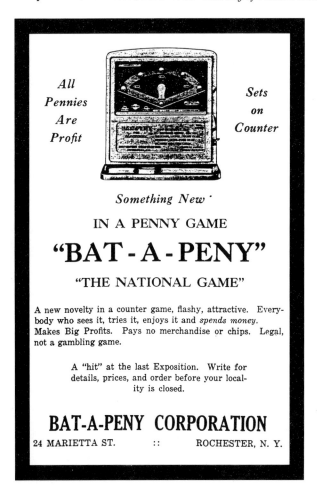

Advertisement for Bat-A-Peny.

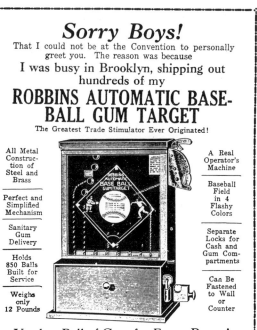

Advertisement for Robbins Automatic Baseball Gum Target. 1928.

Advertisement for Northwest Coin Machine Co.'s Base Ball Wonder, 1931. *Courtesy of Phill Emmert.*

Advertisement for Texas Leaguer. *Courtesy of Phill Emmert.*

The Keeney Texas Leaguer copies many of the features of Atlas Indicator Works game, and was very popular in its day. Few examples remain today, particularly with an original stand. *Courtesy of William Howard.*

Close-up view of Keeney's Texas Leaguer. *Courtesy of Howard Pollack, M.D.*

Keeny's League Leader, 1940. Ball comes down the ramp and is hit with the bat. 6' x 6.5' x 2.5'. *Courtesy of Howard Pollack, M.D.*

151

A unique arcade game (which could also be considered a vending machine) was the 1947 Victor Vending Home Run. It came on a stand an had a gambling feature. It rewarded the player if he could maneuver his gum ball into a home run slot while fighting the laws of gravity. *Courtesy of William Howard.*

Mexican Baseball coin-op. 20" x 13". *From the Cooper collection.*

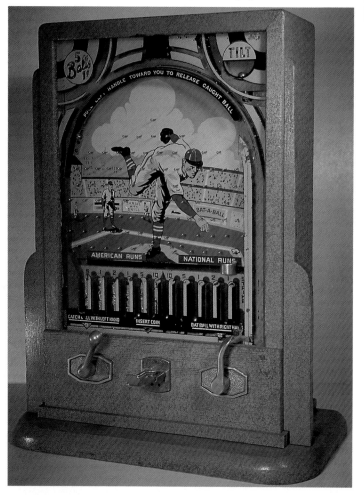

The Junior League Bat-A-Ball, 1930s, has wonderful graphics. *Courtesy of William Howard.*

H.C. Evans advertisement for Bat A Score. *Courtesy of Phill Emmert.*

152

Rock-ola 1937 World Series. The number one arcade game, desired by all baseball and arcade collectors. At the top is a cut glass marquee which says 1937 World Series. This was the only year that this was made, but it copied the earlier All-American Baseball game produced by Amusement Machine Corporation *From the Cooper collection.*

Evan's Bat-A-Score. Electro-mechanical pinball coin-op. Hitting a ball into the tiers in the back determined whether you hit a single, double, triple, or home run. *Courtesy of Mike Brown.*

Home Run. Penny arcade game where the pistol shoots the ball at a target. If you hit the home run bulls eye you get a gum ball. c. 1930s. *Courtesy of Mike Brown.*

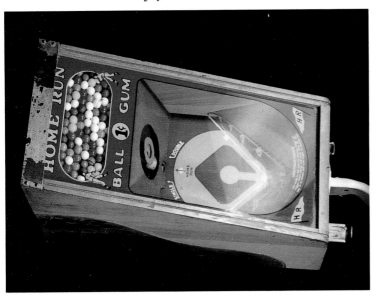

As the players make outs the next player's name shows up in the batter up box. *From the Cooper collection.*

153

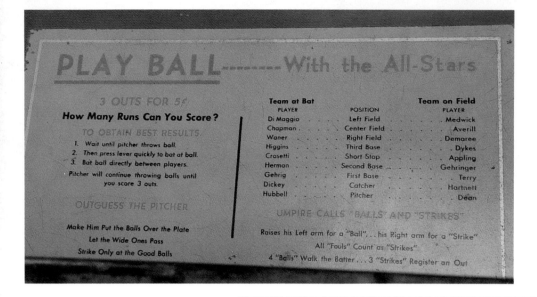

The line-ups of the National and American League players from the 1937 World Series in the lower left playing field. *From the Cooper collection.*

The playing field. The outfielders move from side to side as the game is played. *From the Cooper collection.*

A close-up of the players. The All-Star decal is supposed to be across the chest of the uniform. *From the Cooper collection.*

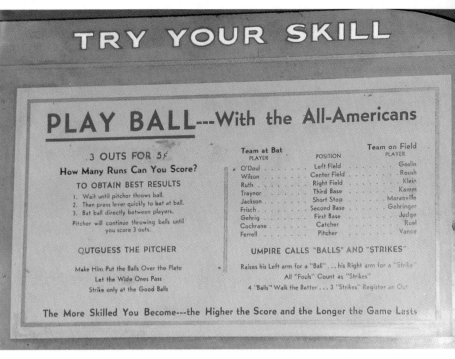

PLAY BASE BALL
The AMERICAN BASE BALL GAME

TRY YOUR SKILL

PLAY BALL---With the All-Americans

3 OUTS FOR 5¢

How Many Runs Can You Score?

TO OBTAIN BEST RESULTS
1. Wait until pitcher throws ball.
2. Then press lever quickly to bat at ball.
3. Bat ball directly between players.
Pitcher will continue throwing balls until you score 3 outs.

OUTGUESS THE PITCHER

Make Him Put the Balls Over the Plate
Let the Wide Ones Pass
Strike only at the Good Balls

Team at Bat		Team on Field
PLAYER	POSITION	PLAYER
O'Doul	Left Field	Goslin
Wilson	Center Field	Roush
Ruth	Right Field	Klein
Traynor	Third Base	Kamm
Jackson	Short Stop	Maranville
Frisch	Second Base	Gehringer
Gehrig	First Base	Judge
Cochrane	Catcher	Ruel
Ferrell	Pitcher	Vance

UMPIRE CALLS "BALLS" AND "STRIKES"

Raises his Left arm for a "Ball" . . . his Right arm for a "Strike"
All "Fouls" Count as "Strikes"
4 "Balls" Walk the Batter . . . 3 "Strikes" Register an Out

The More Skilled You Become---the Higher the Score and the Longer the Game Lasts

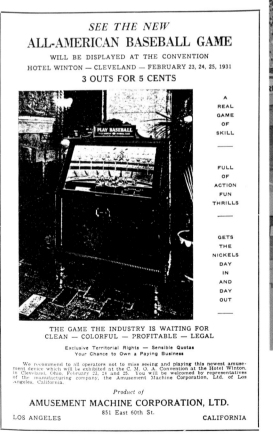

A 1931 advertisement for the All-American Baseball Game.
Courtesy of Phill Emmert.

The All-American Baseball Game. The original arcade game from the 1920s that Rockola copied for its 1937 World Series game. As you can see the playing field is almost identical. The line-up has all the stars from the 1920s, whereas the Rockola game had the starting line-up from the 1937 All-Star game. The earlier version used a more colorful gallery. Amusement Machine Corporation, Ltd.

BREAKING ALL RECORDS—
CHESTER-POLLARD BASEBALL GAMES

The Masterpiece of Sport Machines has been accepted by New York's leading hotels and is proving the greatest money-earner of any mechanical game ever installed in these important locations. Hotels and Clubs throughout the U. S. and Canada are anxiously awaiting installations.

Played as Real Baseball Is Played

The Reasons Why The Game Is a Masterpiece:

No. 1—The Pitcher delivers the ball to the Batter. Unless the Batter connects with the delivery, it is a ball or strike. If four balls are delivered, the batter "walks" to first base.

No. 2—The Batter may bunt or hit the ball hard. When running to bases the runner's progress is shown by a series of little lights along the base paths.

No. 3—The Fielders stop the ball and return it to the base where the play is to be made. Should the ball reach the base in time to head off the runner, an out is registered.

No. 4—The Score Board registers each out, strike and run.

No. 5—Other features: A runner can steal bases; the ball can be knocked over the bleachers for a home run, and, in fact, every play can be made as in the actual game of baseball.

Chester-Pollard Amusement Co., Inc.

Manufacturers of the Successful Football, Golf and Derby Games, the Balloon Racer, Kentucky Derby and Cony (Rabbit) Race.

188 West Fourth Street   New York City

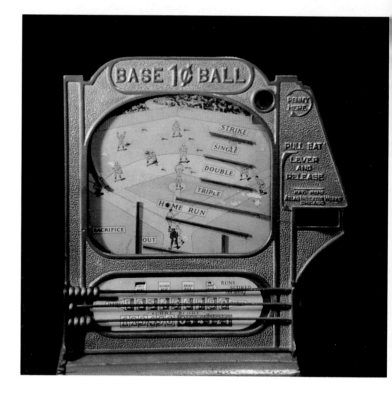

Atlas Indicator Work Baseball Game, paint variation. Wood and metal, 13" x 12" x 7.5". *Courtesy of Mike Brown.*

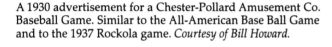

A 1930 advertisement for a Chester-Pollard Amusement Co. Baseball Game. Similar to the All-American Base Ball Game and to the 1937 Rockola game. *Courtesy of Bill Howard.*

Rockola 1934 World Series mechanical pinball machine. It stood on legs and originally was painted battleship gray. 36" x 17". *From the Cooper collection.*

Pinball

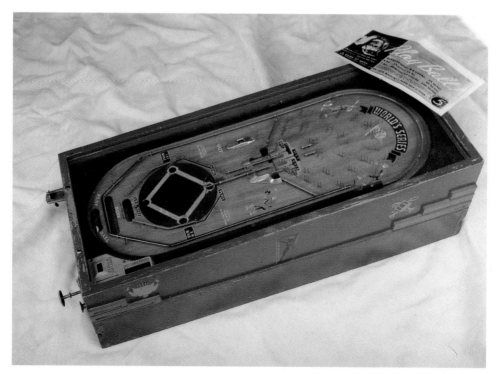

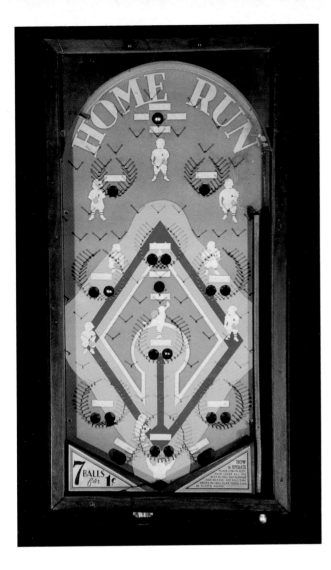

Home Run. Bagatelle tabletop game with seven balls for one cent. The destination of the ball determined the outcome. 1930s. *Courtesy of Mike Brown.*

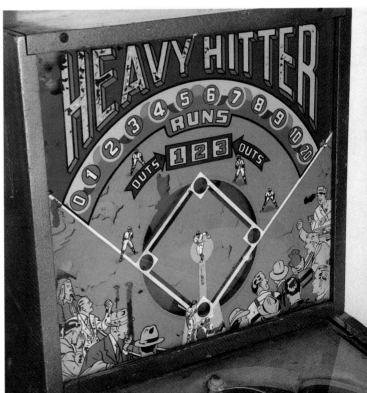

Heavy Hitter, late 1940s. A half-sized representation of a contemporary electro-mechanical pinball machine. There are hundreds of baseball pinball machines, however, they are beyond the scope of this book. L 34" x W 15" x H 25". *From the Cooper collection.*

MAJOR LEAGUE

IS AMAZING·OPERATORS WITH ITS TREMENDOUS EARNINGS...

TAKE ON A WINNER!

You can believe me, boys, when I say that MAJOR LEAGUE is going to be one of the biggest money makers for many months to come! That's why I'm ready to deliver as soon as I receive your order. Come on, fellows—let's go!

ORDER IMMEDIATELY FROM JOE!

Advertisement for the Major League pinball machine by the Vending Machine Co., Fayetteville, North Carolina. *Courtesy of Bill Howard.*

Bambino, 1938. Full body art work of Babe Ruth on the playing field, with a player sliding inot the catcher as the upper half. Five balls for a nickel, with ball kickers on each side of the playing field for triples and homeruns. Contact with the playing field coils advances runners. *Courtesy of Roger Burbank.*

All Stars, 1936. This game has a master coil in the back that changes the odds. Thirty nickels is the maximum payout, with a two nickel minimum. Art work on the playing field is beautiful, with banners of the 1936 teams. The game also has a split feature where you get half the payout, and a double header feature, which gives you your ball back. Bally. *Courtesy of Roger Burbank.*

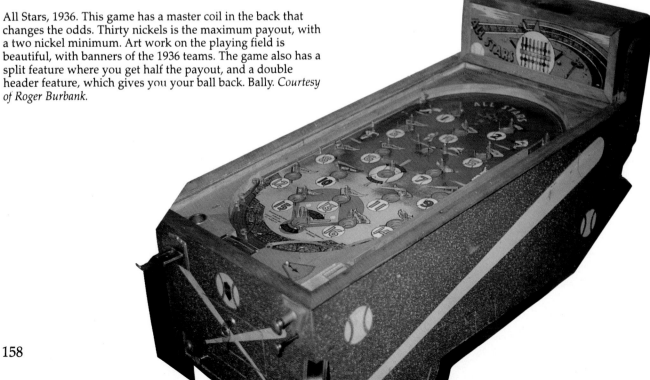

Index to Games

Price Guide

The price guide reflects retail prices of games in excellent condition. Complete games are obviously more valuable than incomplete games. When a range is given, it reflects a game that can be purchased between the upper limit of the lower range and the lower limit of the upper. For example, D-E means a price somewhere between $900-1400. Auction prices, I believe, do not necessarily reflect the average retail price. By their nature price guides are inaccurate. The author and publisher assume no responsibility for gain or loss from its use.

Position Codes

T = Top   TL = Top Left   BR = Bottom Right
C = Center   TC = Top Center   CL = Center left
B = Bottom   TR = Top Right   CR = Center right
R = Right   BL = Bottom Left   L = Left
       BC = Bottom Center

Price Codes

A = $50-150

B = $150-300

C = $300-600

D = $600-1000

E = $1000-2500

F = $2500-5000

G = $5000-10000

H = Over $10000

Page	Pos.	Price	Page	Pos.	Price	Page	Pos.	Price
67	TL	D	94	TL	B-C	126	TL	C
67	B	D	94	TR	A	126	TR	B
68	TL	A	94	BL	A	126	BR	B
68	CR	A	94	BR	A	127		D-E
68	BL	A-B	95	T	B-C	128	T	C
69	TL	A-B	95	B	A	128	BL	B
69	BL	B	96	TL	B	128	BR	C
70	TL	B	96	CL	B	129	TL	B
70	CR	A	96	CR	B	129	TR	B
70	BL	A	96	BR	B	129	BL	B
71	TL	C	97	TL	A-B	129	BR	A
71	CR	B	97	TR	A-B	130	TR	D-E
71	BL	B	97	CL	C	130	CL	E
72	TL	D-E	97	CR	A	130	BR	A
72	TR	C	97	BL	A-B	131	TL	B
72	CR	E	98	TL	B	131	TR	B
72	BL	B	98	CR	A	131	BL	B
73	CR	A	98	CL	B-C	132	TL	B
73	BL	D-E	98	BR	A-B	132	TR	B
74	TL	B	99	TL	B-C	132	BL	B
74	CR	A	99	CR	A-B	132	BR	B
74	BL	A-B	99	BL	A	133	TL	A
75	TL	A	100	TL	A-B	133	TR	A
75	CR	A	100	CR	B	133	BL	B
75	BL	A	100	BL	A	134	TL	A
76	T	A-B	101	TL	B	134	TR	A
76	CL	A	101	CR	A-B	134	BL	A
76	CR	A	101	BL	A-B	134	BR	A
76	BR	A	102	TR	A-B	135	TL	A
77	TL	A	102	BL	C	135	TR	A
77	CR	A	102	BR	A	135	B	A
77	BL	A	103	TL	A-B	136	TL	A
78	T	C	103	TR	A-B	136	TR	A
78	B	B	103	BL	A	136	BR	C-D
79	TR	A-B	103	BR	A	137	TR	F
79	CL	A	104	T	A-B	137	BR	G-H
79	BR	A-B	104	CL	A	138	TL	D
80	TL	A-B	104	BR	A	138	BL	F
80	CR	A	105	TL	A	139	TL	F-G
80	BL	A	105	CR	B	139	BR	G
81	TL	B	105	BL	A	140	BL	F-G
81	TR	B	106	TR	A-B	140	BR	D
81	BL	B	107	CR	A	141	CR	E
81	BR	B	108	CL	A	141	BL	E
82	TR	B	108	BR	A	142		D-E
82	CL	D	109	TL	A	143	TL	F-G
82	R	B	109	BR	A	143	BL	F
83	TL	D	109	CL	A	144	TL	D
83	TR	A	109	CR	A-	144	TR	D
83	BL	C-D	110	TR	A-	144	BR	D
83	BR	D	111	CL	A	145	TL	D
84	T	D	112	BR	A-	145	TR	C
85	TL	B	115	TL	B	145	BL	D
85	R	B	115	BL	A	145	BR	E
85	BL	A	115	BR	E-F	146	TL	D-E
86	TL	B	116	TL	B	146	TR	C
86	CR	D-E	116	TR	B	146	BL	D-E
86	BL	E	116	BL	A-B	146	BR	D
87	TL	C	116	BR	A-B	147	TL	D
87	TR	A	117	TL	E-F	147	TR	C-D
87	BL	B	117	BL	B	147	BL	D
87	BR	C-D	118	TL	B-C	147	BR	C
88	TR	B	118	TR	E	148	TL	D
88	CL	B-C	118	BL	B	148	TR	C
88	B	A	118	BR	E	148	BR	C
89	TL	A	119	TL	B	149	TL	D
89	TR	B	119	CR	A	149	TR	F-G
89	BL	B-C	119	BL	E	149	BR	E-F
89	BR	B	120	TL	A	150	TL	E
90	TL	B-C	120	CR	B	151	TL	D-E
90	TR	A	120	BL	B	151	BR	D-E
90	BL	B-C	121	TL	A	152	TL	D
90	BR	A	121	BL	D	152	TR	D
91	TL	B	121	BR	A	152	BL	D-E
91	TR	B	122	TL	B	153	TL	F
91	BL	C-D	122	CR	A-B	153	TR	G
92	TC	C	122	BL	A	154		H
92	BL	B-C	123	TL	C	155	TR	D-E
92	BR	C	123	CR	A	155	BR	D-E
93	TL	B	123	BL	B	156	TL	D
93	TR	A	124	TL	B	156	TR	D
93	CR	B-C	124	BR	B-C	157	TR	E
93	BL	A	125		F	157	BR	E

Page	Pos.	Price	Page	Pos.	Price
21	B	H	47		D-E
23		H	48	TC	E
28	TL	F-G	48	CR	D-E
29	TL	F-G	48	BL	D-E
29	CR	D-E	49		F
30		E	50	TR	C
31	TR	F	50	BL	C
31	BL	F-G	50	BR	D
32	T	E	51	TL	D-E
32	BR	E	51	TR	B-C
33	TL	D	51	BL	D
33	BL	E	51	BR	C-D
34	TR	D	52	TL	E-F
34	CL	E	52	BR	C
35	TL	D-E	53	TL	C
35	BL	D-E	53	B	E
36	TL	E	54	TR	D
36	TR	D	54	BL	E-F
36	B	D	55	T	D
37	TL	D	55	B	C
37	TR	C	56	T	C-D
37	BL	C-D	56	B	D-E
38	TL	E	57	TL	D
38	TR	E	57	CR	D
38	B	D	57	BL	B-C
39	TL	E-F	58	TL	D
39	BL	D-E	58	TR	D
40	TL	D	58	B	D
40	CR	D	59	TL	C
40	BL	B-C	59	CR	D
40	BR	E	59	BL	C-D
41	TL	D	60	TL	B
41	CR	D-E	60	B	C
42		E	61	TL	E
43	TL	E	61	BL	A
43	TR	E	61	BR	B-C
43	BL	E	62	TL	B-C
44	TL	B	62	TR	B
44	TR	C-D	63	TL	C-D
44	CR	E	63	BL	D-E
44	BL	C	64	TR	A
44	BR	C	64	CL	A
45		C (cardbox)	64	BR	A
45		C-D (Lawson brown)	65	T	B-C
			65	B	D-E
46	TR	E	66	TR	B
46	CL	G	66	CL	C-D
46	BR	F-G	66	BR	D